walking IN MY SON'S *footsteps*

HARMOHAN SINGH

walking IN MY SON'S *footsteps*

david's fight for freedom

Copyright © 2020 by Harmohan Singh.

All rights reserved. No part of this book may be used or reproduced in any manner whatsoever without prior written consent of the author, except as provided by the United States of America copyright law.

Published by Thinktosee Press.

Printed in the United States of America.

10 9 8 7 6 5 4 3 2 1

ISBN: 978-1-94963-953-7
LCCN: 2019917269

Book design by Megan Elger

This publication is designed to provide accurate and authoritative information in regard to the subject matter covered. It is sold with the understanding that the publisher is not engaged in rendering legal, accounting, or other professional services. If legal advice or other expert assistance is required, the services of a competent professional person should be sought.

For David:
You will always be my life.

CONTENTS

ACKNOWLEDGMENTS.................... ix

CHAPTER 1........................... 1
Introduction to David

CHAPTER 2 27
David's Childhood

CHAPTER 3 45
David the Artist and Scholar

CHAPTER 4 65
David the Young Man

CHAPTER 5........................... 81
David's Politics, Philosophy, and Spirituality

CHAPTER 6 99
David's Depression and Psychiatry in Singapore

CHAPTER 7.......................... 117
Answers and Activism for David

CHAPTER 8 155
Brainwashing a Nation: How Singapore's Culture Hurts Children and Families

CHAPTER 9 175
How to Help a Teen Who May Be Suicidal—Advice
for Friends, Parents, and Educators

CONCLUSION 191

POSTSCRIPT. 195

ACKNOWLEDGMENTS

There are many good folks who were so helpful and generous with their love, support, and contributions to the commission of this book. Without them, David's story would never be, and I, his father, would have failed him—yet again and miserably.

David's sister, Sara, will always be my guiding light. She, in our time of tragedy and crisis, shared her strength and faith so I could go on with the mission that David left to us.

David's uncle Harbajan and aunt Daisy, who stood by us throughout and whose love and guidance helped energize me. Also, friends whom I had known most of my adult life were by our side—Jerry and Celine, Rick and Made, and Mel and Patricia. From them, I understood the meaning of friendship.

David's friends and teachers were an invaluable part of the story. Their accounts speak for themselves—of the deepest friendship, respect, and dreams that they shared. I felt their loss immeasurably. How they loved David: Kimberly, Kat, Caroline, Liz, Madeleine, Simren, Verena, Meera, Agnes, Christina, Tiffany, Li Ying, Marilyn, Larissa, Zylphia, Nicole, Claudine, Jen, Angelique, Xin Yi, Mrs. Bull, Audrey, Elsa, Mrs. Ng, Chris, Kieran, Hamssini, Debbie, Lesha, Elizabeth, Gina, Joann, Eleanor, Tessa, Dinithi, Julia, Eva, Laura, Sean, Ben, Mrs. Rao, and many more.

Trevor Rodrigues, Gaynor Fitzgibbon, Maria Santelli, Cameran Clayton, and also the folks at Infinitas SJII were most loving with their contributions about David in their respective newsletters.

Ching and Magdalene, Clay and Surene, and Professor and Mrs. Ong were just a few of the parents of David's friends who were most supportive throughout.

Edna, who helped to care for David and who happily bore the brunt of many of his practical jokes in our home. Mary, who kept him company when David accompanied me to work.

Ariel, Elaine, Josh, Megan, and the folks at Advantage| ForbesBooks, whose generous help I came to rely on for the commission of this book.

From David's paternal grandmother, Kishen, I learned one of life's greatest lessons—perseverance.

To each one of you, David's family thanks you. For those whom I may have inadvertently missed mentioning, your loving support was no less appreciated. Thank you too.

Finally, from David, whom this book is dedicated to, I learned the greatest lesson of all: Fight! For justice.

—David's father
www.thinktosee.tumblr.com

Ours have been a history of war.

This is for the countless who

Refuse to let our future be so.

—David C. Singh

You smug faced crowds with kindling eye

Who cheer when soldier lads march by,

Sneak home and pray you'll never know

The hell where youth and laughter go.

—Siegfried Sassoon

Do not silence me.

Let my work live.

Do not fail me, again.

—David C. Singh

David left these messages on his bed for me that fateful day …

LEGACY

By David Cornelius Singh

Hope?
A rock, a guardian, a keeper, a protector, hero?
There are two versions of a hero,
One you commemorate, you aspire to be,
And one you love, you aspire to push,
who protects you
A keeper to my heart, is the cost of your devotion,
The only holder of the key, and the only hero,
whom I love, and protects me.

—David Cornelius Singh
(found at the end of his black book, titled *Human*, containing his poems, plays, and sketches)

CHAPTER 1

Introduction to David

It was February 24 of 2015—the final year that my son, David, was in high school. It was our routine that every day I drove him to school in the morning. Along the way we would stop and pick up one of his schoolmates, Gina Woodmansee, who lived nearby. One day—for what exact reason, I can't remember—she did not join us. When we arrived at the usual spot where I dropped him off, David handed me a letter, saying simply, "This is for you."

Watching him walk up to the school that day, I knew immediately this was not good news—David never gave me letters.

After leaving the school, I pulled to the side of the road and sat there wondering whether I should open the letter now or later. Deciding it was better to go ahead and deal with it, I opened the envelope; inside was a letter in which David told me he was going to be drafted for military service the following year, 2016. This much I knew already; the laws of Singapore dictated it.

In the letter David also said that he was not going to allow himself to be drafted. He indicated that he was quite prepared—if it came to this—to take his life.

Naturally, as I read this, I was tremendously concerned—devastated, really. Frankly, I didn't know what to do. My son had always been what you could call a good boy. Just like his older sister, Sara, he had been easy to raise. I had custody of my two children, but I never experienced any of the frightful behavioral issues you hear of single parents enduring; Sara and David never gave me any problems growing up. This was the first major challenge I had experienced with David, and I felt instantly that it was an issue my family needed to come together to solve.

In the simplest of terms, his problem was this: he didn't want to go into the army. I needed help navigating the legalese of conscription law in order to determine what I could do for my son, so I turned to my eldest brother, Harbajan Singh, who is a lawyer. Harbajan had always been a mentor of sorts to me. My senior by thirteen years, he was, in a sense, more of a father to me than my own father had been.

Although my children's mother and I were divorced, having separated in 2006, I decided that I needed to inform her of this struggle. I informed my brother of this decision. So I called and explained to her that I needed to see her urgently about David. She asked what it was about, but I declined to discuss it on the phone. She has faced, and continues to struggle with, many obstacles of her own, which are not mine to delve into, so suffice it to say that she did not seem up to this challenge. From my conversation with her, I understood that any decisions about this situation were mine to make.

My first decision along these lines was to broach this anxious matter head on. That afternoon at 3:15 p.m., I went to fetch David from school, and then, the moment he got in the car, right away I said, "Look, I read your letter." I asked him if he wanted to see a counselor.

He replied, "Yes."

"Okay. Let's get you a counselor and see whether we can address your concerns."

Fortunately, Harbajan was able to put us in touch with a psychiatrist he knew. I initiated the contact, and we made an appointment for David. The very next week, I accompanied my son to see this doctor. Thereafter, David continued to see him every three or four weeks.

The doctor diagnosed him with clinical depression, for which he prescribed medication. I think the depression was a result of cumulative negative experiences over the course of his childhood and adolescent years (e.g., witnessing his parents' divorce and believing it was his fault, even though it certainly was not; being gay in a society that rejects and criminalizes homosexuality; etc.).

As his father, I understood that the most looming aspect of his depression stemmed from feeling stuck in a rigid system that demanded not only that he acted a certain way but also that he bought into its ideology and made sacrifices for it—namely, conscription. I knew this generated a great deal of fear and anxiety for him. As a consequence of David's interest in subjects such as theater and literature, he had shared and developed certain views of the world: he believed in nonviolence and considered himself a conscientious objector.

I wholly supported my son in this matter. Nothing could

> *As his father, I understood that the most looming aspect of his depression stemmed from feeling stuck in a rigid system that demanded not only that he acted a certain way but also that he bought into its ideology and made sacrifices for it—namely, conscription.*

have given me more pride than witnessing him strive to make the world a better place for everyone in a peaceful, loving way.

Over the next few months, as David continued with his final year in school and underwent treatment for his depression, I began to feel hesitantly confident that the matter was under control. Still, in the back of my mind, I knew that the critical period—the one that would truly decide things—would come after school was finished at year's end. At that time, he would have only a month or two before he was conscripted.

It was heartening to see that everything went on as normal at home: David was his customary playful, naughty self. He has always been a fan of witty retorts and practical jokes, and both continued in full force within our home.

I did not see anything different with his schoolwork either. At his private school, St. Joseph's Institution International (SJII), he had always been a motivated A-student who excelled in science, math, and the arts, turning in exemplary projects and exams. His senior year proved no exception. On his Swiss-administered International Baccalaureate (IB) exam, David scored forty-four out of a possible total of forty-five points, meaning that for each of the seven subjects he had studied in school, he earned an A on the exam.

In the coming chapters, I will go into detail about both David's lower-grade schooling (a markedly different environment, one in which he was *not* the motivated student he later turned out to be) and high school, in which he developed his scholarly and artistic aptitudes. I will also focus on his friends in school. David was gay, and most of his friends turned out to be girls, though his friend Kimi insists that his sexuality didn't really have anything to do with their friendship. In fact, she didn't know he was gay until after knowing him for quite some time, and she liked him, as she told me, for "his personality and just who he is, his humor and kindness." They could relate to him and he to them, and from their commonalities flourished several beautiful, familial friendships. It is sufficient for now to say that going into his senior year, David was academically strong and surrounded by supportive friends and teachers. These factors did not change throughout his twelfth-grade year—even after I received his worrisome letter.

At the time of his graduation, David had recently had a falling-out of sorts with his mother. I was not privy to the details of it—it was between them—but I do know it reached a point that he did not wish to invite her to the ceremony. In fact, I still have the text message he sent me asking if he could stop seeing her.

While I had generally allowed David to set his own course and make even the larger decisions for himself, this was not something I could condone. Going against his wishes—something I rarely did—I invited his mother to see him graduate. "Look," I said to him, "no matter what, she's still your mother, and I'm going to invite her." I had thought long and hard about this. It was a once-in-a-lifetime experience, and I didn't feel it was fair for his mother to miss it.

This occasion was of such importance in our family that David's sister, Sara, flew in from Australia, where she was doing university. His mother sat separately from us, although I invited her to join us; she felt more comfortable sitting elsewhere.

Immediately after the graduation came one of the most touching scenes I've experienced with my son. Even though he disagreed with my decision to invite his mother, and even though he would later chastise me for it, David approached me when the ceremony was complete and handed me his diploma. He said to me, "This is for you."

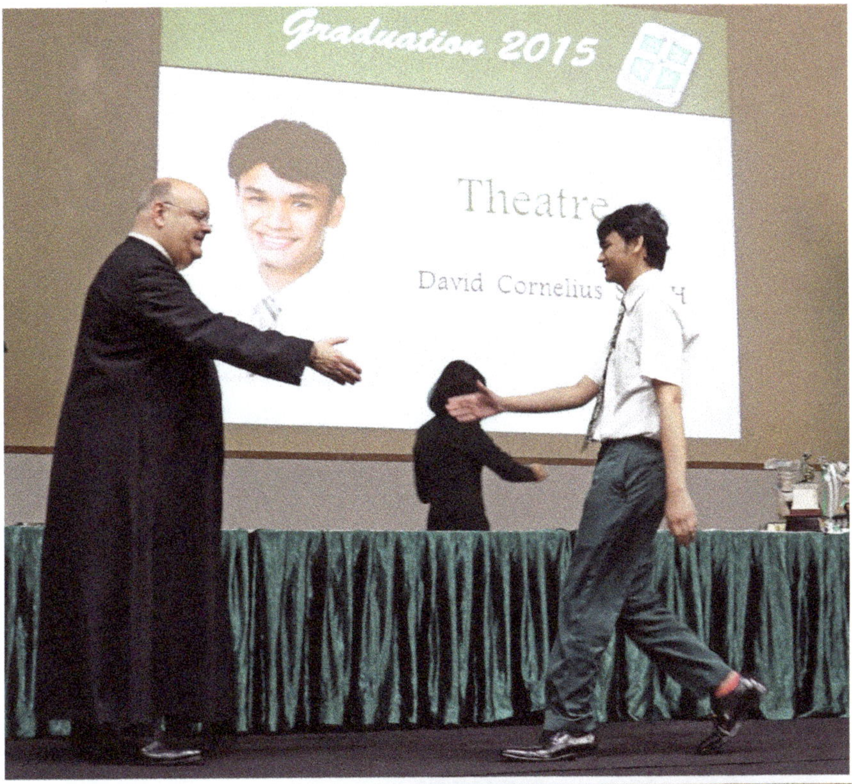
Graduation 2015
Theatre
David Cornelius

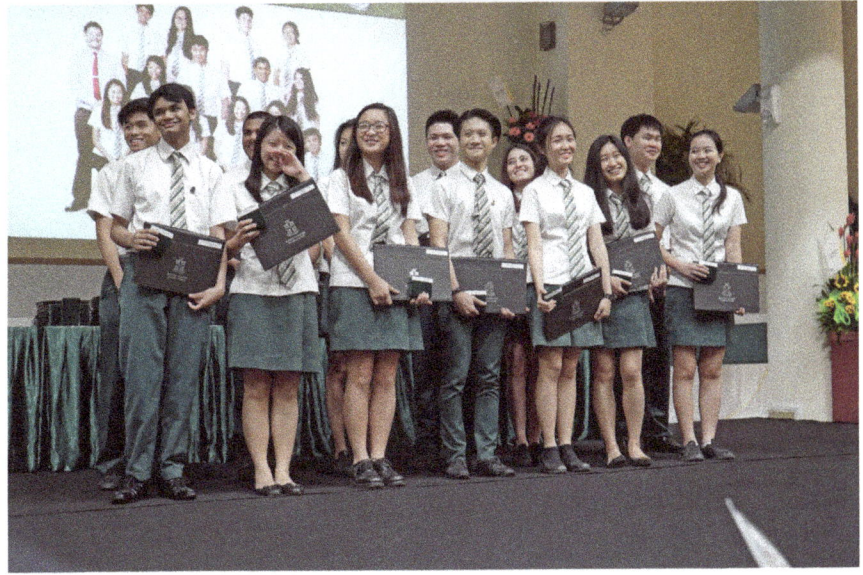

Knowing how hard David had worked to propel himself to this point—graduating with outstanding educational credits, along with a prestigious theater award—I felt profoundly moved. It was rewarding beyond words to see him accomplish all that he had and equally gratifying that he chose to honor me in that moment. I am eternally grateful to my son for this gesture.

After his graduation, he had a few months before he would be conscripted. In the meantime, we continued working with the psychiatrist. A letter was drafted to the proper channels within the armed forces informing them that David had been diagnosed with clinical depression, and that in his current condition, he was not fit for normal military service.

In response to this, the armed forces downgraded him to a desk job. When I first learned of this, I considered it a step in the right direction, and I hoped David would view it in the same light. This was a relief not so much because David wouldn't be on the front lines of danger—Singapore was not involved in any conflict at the time—but because a desk job seemed less at odds with his views about war and military.

I said to David, "The armed forces say they downgraded you. Isn't that good?"

"It's not good enough," he replied. Then he explained to me that no matter what position they put him in—clerk, driver, or anything else—he would still be enabling a violent system that he adamantly opposed.

He had his own ideas about how we could remedy the situation. "Please," he pleaded with me, "take me away."

I always heard David out. "Where you would like to go?" I asked him.

New York was the first place he named. He had visited there twice already, and NYU was one of the two major schools he was considering for college; he was interested in studying dramatic writing there. To him, New York was an iconic city. The theater! The freedom!

I gave this due thought, but it occurred to me that if I were to take him away, two things would happen. Number one, he would be breaking the law here by evading military service. Number two, when his passport expired, they would not renew it for him—he would be stuck as an illegal alien in America.

While part of me desperately wanted to do exactly as he asked and take him away, these were legitimate concerns. I didn't know what to do. Visions of my son locked in a detention center with other illegal aliens loomed in my thoughts.

During the school holidays, starting in November 2015 and running all the way through February of the following year, David mostly stayed home. For someone who loved traveling and seeing new places, David now showed no interest in trips—not even to see his sister in Australia.

At some point I earnestly tried to convince him to break out of his routine at home and collect some one-of-a-kind experiences with his friends. To my surprise, David agreed. He told me that in January, he and a bunch of his friends were going to take a trip to Hong Kong.

I took this as wonderful news. David was well traveled, knowledgeable, and mature enough that for him to go on such a trip unchaperoned was no cause for concern. I was relieved to see a resurgence of some of his previous interest in travel. So it was with a lighter heart that I watched him head off with three of his girlfriends, Caroline Yap, Kimi Cheah, and Kat Lee, to Hong Kong, where they spent six days.

In January 2016, David came back from this vacation seemingly in lighter spirits. His improved mood seemed to attest that he had only needed to get out and spend more time with people—and to have a reprieve from his anxiety about military service.

Around this same time, Edna, our housekeeper, returned to her home in the Philippines for the holidays. She was gone from December 9, 2015, to February 9, 2016. This meant that, for some time, David and I were alone in the house.

Singapore being a primarily Chinese society, we celebrate the Lunar New Year here. In early February, everyone all around us was preparing for it. Here, the Lunar New Year is equivalent to Thanksgiving or Christmas in the United States, and because David and Sara were Chinese on their mother's side, they had always participated in the celebration with enthusiasm. David in particular had always been excited about the holiday, but for the last few years he had avoided going to his maternal grandparents' home, where we traditionally celebrated. He got along well with his grandparents (especially his grandmother, who clearly considered David her favorite grandchild), but I believe his feelings about going there were complicated by his feelings toward his mother.

When it came time for the Lunar New Year, I asked him, as I always did, whether he planned on going to see his mother and grandparents. He shook his head. He wanted nothing to do with it.

"Has your mother called you?" I asked.

"No."

"Okay then," I told him, not pushing the matter further. I didn't know what to do, though; the Lunar New Year is typically a large family festival. I had hoped David would be up to participating, and that this experience, like his trip to Hong Kong with his friends, would revive his spirits.

It was in early February when he declined to ring in the Lunar New Year with his family. Then came February 14, 2016—a Sunday—two days before he was to be conscripted. On this day, a friend invited me for coffee and a chat. He and his wife were the parents of one of Sara's former classmates, and they knew David, so I invited David to come along.

David told me he didn't feel like going out, so I went out for a few minutes to the coffee shop to get him *roti prata*, an Indian breakfast that he loved. I got home and served it to him and then went on my way. Edna had the day off and had left in the morning, so David was on his own while I was gone. I met with my friend about lunchtime; when I returned home at approximately two o'clock, I noticed David was still in the house. I observed him going in and out of his room, watching a TV program, I believe. His behavior seemed routine; there was nothing occurring to arouse my suspicion. I brought him lunch and then retired to my bedroom to read for a little while. After a short time, I noticed he had not touched his lunch, so I knocked on his door and said, "David, please take your lunch." When I returned to my room, I heard the sound of ordinary movements from his room—the sounds of his coming out, the door slamming, his walking back into his room, that kind of thing.

It was perhaps an hour after that when I noticed that he still had not touched his lunch. When I went to his room this time, I noticed the door was locked. In the hall I kept a set of keys to all the doors in the house—I hurried for it. When I opened the door, I saw him sitting by the window. And I knew I had lost him.

I tried to revive him. I tried mouth-to-mouth resuscitation, putting pressure on his chest, all the first aid I knew. But it was too late. I was too late. I called the emergency services number, hoping against hope the paramedics could somehow revive him. During this time, Edna got home from her day off and saw me trying to revive David. She went into shock. She should never have had to see that. No one should.

David left a message on his bed explaining why he had done this, laid out eloquently across a collection of twenty-five poems along with a few plays. It was a prodigious volume of work that, piece by piece, expressed his powerful beliefs, his objections, his emotions.

As you will see in later chapters, David won writing competitions, published his work, and received a great deal of acclaim for this skill.

The letter he'd left me was sealed. I did not want to open it yet, but I also did not want the police seeing it before I'd read it; I put it aside for the time being. I began the long, laborious, and exceptionally painful process of doing *what one did* after losing a loved one, all the while being aware I was in shock.

When I finally opened the envelope in the presence of the police investigator in our home, I found a two-page, typewritten poem titled "Voyage." At the top, David had written,

Do not silence me.
Let my work live.
Do not fail me, again.

A few weeks later, while finally summoning the energy to go through his personal belongings, I found the black book, titled *Human*. There was a simple note inside. "Promise me you'll be happy," it read.

I began the long, laborious, and exceptionally painful process of doing what one did after losing a loved one, all the while being aware I was in shock.

* * *

In the chapters that follow, I will describe in detail David's character, interests, and activities at various stages of life, calling on firsthand accounts from his many close friends, as well as his teachers and relatives. However, it is important to know a few things about David up front.

From the time he was very young, he was primarily an idealist. This is an easy thing to call oneself, and as it denotes a desirable characteristic, it's the sort of label many people affix to themselves. David was different. There was no artifice in his idealism; it was not some abstract quality that barely infringed on his day-to-day living. What David said is exactly what he meant. If he said he wasn't going to do something, that was it—he wasn't going to be persuaded otherwise.

I recall a good example of this from when David was ten years old. Just as I equipped him with good instruction of the mind, I wanted him to strengthen his body as well. As swimming was excellent exercise—and an activity David already enjoyed—I started him on swimming lessons.

Well, it turned out he indeed liked swimming, but only as pure recreation—not under instruction. He came to me saying he didn't want to do it anymore, and at first I rejected his request to quit, saying, "No, it's good for you; you need to stick with it."

The following Sunday he headed for his swimming lessons at the pool on the first level of our condominium—or so I thought. Shortly I received a call from the coach asking where David was. "Isn't he at the pool with you?" I asked. He had not shown up.

After telling the instructor I would find out what was going on, I found Edna, our housekeeper, and asked if she knew where David was. She did not, but together the two of us searched the whole estate and beyond, until finally we found him at the playground about a mile away. He was sitting on a swing by himself.

"I told you I didn't want to go swimming anymore," he pointed out. "It's just no fun if someone is making me do it and telling me what to do."

I could tell he was going to stick to his point, and I could not convince him otherwise. What else could I say? "Okay, you made your point. You can forget about swimming. Let's go on home." And that was the end of swimming.

That's David for you. Even at that tender age, when he made up his mind, nothing anyone could do would convince him to change it.

I now keep a blog titled *Think to See* as a tribute to David, and readers of it will recognize that a certain phrase pops up over and over again: "Be yourself." This was one of David's most popular mantras and a simple summary of the principle that guided his life.

Through his spoken words, creative output, and actions, David was always trying to convey the message that there was no use trying to live as someone else—trying to bend to someone else's ideas or standards.

He always believed in being his natural self, and I think his strict adherence to this creed contributed to his auspicious start in playwriting and poetry. A well-defined, authentic point of view shone through his writing. His talent and strong will were often noted by his teachers, some of whom said they wouldn't be at all surprised to see him become an accomplished professor at the young age of twenty-six or twenty-seven.

Initially, he wanted to be a neurosurgeon. At fifteen, he spent weekends volunteering at the hospital—that's how committed he was to anything that interested him. But a year later, he told me he had changed his mind. He had discovered theater, and that's what he wanted to do.

I wasn't sure if that would be good for him, so I asked David to arrange a meeting for us with his theater teacher, Wendy Ng. A few days later, we met in the theater room of the school. "What do you think about this burgeoning interest in theater?" I asked Mrs. Ng.

"Mr. Singh, David is my star student," she said. "I can assure you that he will do very well in his pursuit."

That was enough for me. I immediately turned to David and told him that I would support his passion for theater without reservation. Sometime later, I met David's science teacher at a parent-teacher conference, and she insisted that David should stick with the sciences, as he had great potential. I replied that he had made his choice, and there was no walking back for him. However, he did take a chemistry course for his final year of IB and received an A.

David was equally committed to encouraging his friends to pursue their own passions, which a number of them recalled when reflecting on his memory, including his good friend Marilyn.

David was also one of the most talented, yet humble people I've ever met. A talented actor, who could make any character come to life under the bright lights of the stage. An amazing student, whose insight was greatly valued by everyone. But still, he remained humble. He never put on airs, and always encouraged all of us to be the best we could be.

One incident I remember extremely clearly is when our graduation from SJII neared. The staff put envelopes with our names in our student lounge, and got everyone to write notes of encouragement to one another for us to read on our graduation day. While I still treasure every single letter I received, David's letter really stuck out to me, encouraging me to go for my dreams in his characteristic sassy way.

When we were in grade 12, I was certain that I wanted to study Psychology in University, and I told David that I want to pursue a PhD in said field in the future. And instead of laughing at me for setting such a crazy goal, David jokingly told me in his little note that he "can be one of my research participants when I do my PhD." That one line showed me how much faith David had in me, and looking at that now, two years into my undergraduate degree in Psychology, it reminds me to persevere through the challenges and never give up on that dream.

David's friend Madeleine shared a similar sentiment.

David and I first met in drama class in 2012. It was my second day at the school and the very first class. I still was feeling anxious about not having people to sit with for lunch and other trivial social issues. David simply noticed that I was only talking to my best friend, who had transferred into SJII earlier than me, and not particularly speaking with anyone else. He invited himself to hang out with us during the break afterwards and one can say the rest is history.

Apart from forcing me to study at the national library with him because he knew I wouldn't touch my books at home anyway, David would constantly text me and ask me to hang out and do frivolous activities with him. For instance, I had made brownies for everyone on Valentine's Day, and David didn't like the texture. He made me follow him the very next day after school to a café where he told me to recreate those brownies because those were "substantially better" than mine. Honestly, I was offended. Extremely offended. Given, he hadn't said those comments in front of others, but was it really necessary to prove to me that my teenage skills were no match for professionally made cakes? Looking back, it really was my first brush with the thoughtful side of David, who knew that I probably had more potential than I knew. Sure, it seemed really harsh and the statements he made were almost vicious, but that's how our friendship began and continued to be.

Every time I would attempt to critique a book or theatre piece because I personally did not appreciate an aspect of it, David hurled back dozens of comments about the author, playwright, context, and my sheer lack of appreciation for the arts anyway. Perhaps it is because of this that I cannot stand it when my university peer mates cannot reconcile what we are reading with what is happening back in Singapore.

I must admit that whilst I did not really have many run-ins with the studious side of David, I am glad that I could at least be there to be a friend. One day, when David, Z (my best friend) and I were chilling in town, Z brought up a cute waiter that they had seen in a restaurant. David immediately said we needed to have dinner there that night, and we had to dress up no matter what. He didn't care what day of the week it was, or that it was just a café. He wanted us to "command the stage." He also forced himself to come all the way to my house right before our school dance because he wanted to see my house and my "shrine of men," a term he used to describe my old room where I had put up posters of my favourite singers. He would even join my mother in criticizing me and she would agree with him.

During our IB years, we did not have a single class together, and David would never let me live down dropping drama for chemistry. Even after I got my results, he told me had I taken what I truly liked, I could have been a happier person. It is this advice which I will take to my grave. These two years were when I saw David grow from a stubborn, almost immature, my-way-or-highway person to an even more stubborn person who acknowledged that I was probably not going to change but knew how to respect me for it. He knew that I was stressed with submissions and project work, so he would constantly make me go with him to karaoke, and without me knowing, sometimes extend the time from three to five hours so I couldn't leave on time.

I write about David dragging me around Singapore, but I had my fair share of getting him to go places he didn't want to at first. Such as forcing him to follow me to Sentosa because I just wanted to go to Universal Studios and no one else was free. However, for every "favor" that David did for you, you needed to do him much more back in payment. He made me read tons of reports and critiques that he had written. I had obviously given my feedback only to see him chuck it away in the school bins because it wasn't ready. He was always the perfectionist I wanted to become but will never be able to be. The level of meticulousness that he had is no match for anyone that I know now.

Looking back, if it wasn't for David, I think I would not have been the person I am in university today. He would not be shy to tell me when he was offended by my remarks and would never cease to remind me that some things I said would be extremely offensive because I did not bother learning about the context before using them. He taught me to always think steps ahead of others when trying to solve problems. To always ensure that the solution can last rather than solve the problem at the moment.

David dreamed of going to New York, his favorite city in the world, to pursue his studies. It's unfortunate that we, as adults, oftentimes fail to recognize children's dreams—or fail to recognize their power, at least. Many of us fail to comprehend after we've reached adulthood how sacred a dream is to a young person. It's not something that can be compromised; it's not something that can be negotiated. And it certainly is not something that can be done away with because the military says it's time.

Since David's death, I've been trying to follow up with the armed forces to find out why, given his condition, they did not discharge him entirely. Typically in a situation such as this, he would not have needed to serve. So why did they insist on conscripting him still? Why did they insist he serve?

To my heartbreak, after his passing, I found in his cupboard a play he had written giving a blow-by-blow account of his last interview with the armed forces. This interview had been presented to David and me as an opportunity for military doctors and psychiatrists to evaluate David's fitness for conscription.

I will explain this in some detail in upcoming chapters as well, but what I gleaned immediately from my son's play was that there had been no effort to interview him. Those in the room with him that day had a specific and obvious purpose: to brainwash him into accepting military conscription.

When I read this, I naturally became very upset, and I requested a meeting with the armed forces—a meeting that as of today, they had initially welcomed and then later declined to grant me. We have not once spoken face to face. This is typical armed forces bureaucracy—they make it clear that they have no interest in the lives of their conscripts. While they made attempts to sound accommodating in our early communications ("Yes, we welcome a meeting with you; let's set something up"), weeks would pass with no follow-up. When I pursued the matter, I was treated to one excuse after another; our meeting was always being put off.

It did not take long for me to realize they'd never had any intention whatsoever of meeting with me; eventually an email arrived officially stating that they could not grant my request.

This evasive, self-serving side of the armed forces is something David became well acquainted with before my encounters with them. This is why he reconstructed that final so-called interview as a play and why he asked me to see to it that this play be brought to life. This will be a painful process for me, but it is something I will do—as I will do anything David has requested of me. I understand his reasons all too well: he was treated unethically by the armed forces; it is only right that people be made aware of this.

Just as David planned this regarding the play, it appears he planned out every other detail as well. I would guess that his preparations went on for somewhere between ten months and a year. With one eye always trained on the possibility that the army would not release him, he planned.

As a father, this is perhaps the most painful part of all—observing that my child had to go through so much pain that he found it necessary to plan his own death. This was no impulsive action on David's part; it was carefully mapped out. If they had released him rather than requiring that he be conscripted, I think he would have been all right. I believe David would have gone on to New York, where he would have been happy.

* * *

As time goes by, the pain remains. My deep sorrow is exacerbated by an immeasurable sense of failure as a father, guardian, and caregiver. I was David's shadow. How could the two be separated?

David was always saying, "Life is art and art, life." To understand this statement will require us to look at life without boundaries—with no box to confine our mind and being. This is *freedom*. But let me be clear: it's painful for the shadow to be separated from the being who casts it. I, the shadow, followed the being throughout his young life. I anticipated his every movement, need, and emotion. We were intertwined. We needed each other, mostly to reinforce our senses of identity and thus our security. Every loving parent is this shadow.

Our children are our lives. We nourish our children, and in turn, we are nourished. These are the parameters of our existence. But to the artist, there are no parameters to begin with. The shadow and the being are "separated" only because the former refuses to appreciate that life is much larger than the sum of our mental and physical conditioning. The separation per se is only what we believe it to be within those confines. The shadow and the being can never be separated ... if only we believe, and know. But because our faith as such is not complete, we suffer the pain of separation with this confined space we call our life.

David and his shadow are intertwined eternally!

I would like to share here a beautiful poem written by David, titled "I Love." It vividly captures the essence of David's personality.

I LOVE

Stars tumble today.
A carousel eddies,
Round and round
Dizzying the hot air
Around these porcelain soldiers:
Prehistoric dinosaurs
Hugged from
Some rugged skins, some heroic fronts.

These children, sprouted from struggle,
Crumple as terracotta. Pooled in blood
Their stomachs sip on summer cups,
Make backflips in your winter hearts.

You see, beneath your bombs,
Only the cracked pomegranate:
A cross-section of a massacre
Dotted with ornate arils

Forgetting these refugees,
These tombless shadows clothed black-gold,

Walking arteries, civilian casualties

Are your casual children:

Men and women folded in the static
Of late night monochrome shows.

There, on your carousel,
Listen how the ground tremors
And whispers terror:

"*Ana uhibb!* أحب أنا "

To the amused child on his flaking throne,
The empty pitchers and their money woes;
To the whitened teeth of glossy mosasaur
To their star-less bones.

I may not be the poet my son is, but since his passing, there have been several occasions on which I have found it easiest to express my thoughts through poetry. One of my poems, written on September 27, 2017, describes my purpose going forward in life and in creating this book for and about my dear David. It is titled "Life."

LIFE

For every step I take, it is because of You.
For every vow I make, it is for You.
For every sin I'd done, it is because of Me.
For every tear I shed, it is in memory of You.
For every word you spoke, it is in my heart.

For every father, mother, child ... listen ... listen ... please.

You'll note that, in talking about him, David's friends and family members often refer to him in the present tense, and throughout the book, I will often refer to him this way as well. I frequently employ present tense because David is not part of my past; he is with me always.

CHAPTER 2

David's Childhood

Sara, my firstborn, was the loveliest baby one could imagine. My children's mother, Karen, and I come from different faiths—she is a Roman Catholic and I a Sikh. Children of Sikh households are given the last names Singh for males and Kaur for females; *Singh* means "lion," and *Kaur* means "princess." However, when our first child was born, Karen was adamant that her last name should be Singh. This presented a small problem for me, not only because it went against Sikh tradition but also because it meant my beautiful daughter would not bear the title of princess. Hence, I sought guidance from God and soon received it: Sara! The name means "princess" in Arabic, Hebrew, and Farsi, and to reinforce this, her middle name is Anastasia, in recognition of Princess Anastasia of the Russian royal family the Romanovs.

Four years later, on November 24, 1997, David came along. Once more, I sought guidance from God on a name—and it came four days later: *David*, the King of Israel and Judah, who defeated the giant Goliath in battle. And of course, his last name is Singh—a lion. The Abrahamic faiths recognize King David, too, as a prophet.

David, our son and Sara's brother, was given the middle name Cornelius in honor of a man of peace who had a vision of the higher purpose to which he was called: Cornelius the Centurion was one of the earliest converts to Christianity.

David would go on to more than fulfill the great promise of his name—he would prove himself a courageous peacekeeper, willing and able to stand up to any Goliath. But in his younger years, he was simply a delightful young boy.

> *David would go on to more than fulfill the great promise of his name—he would prove himself a courageous peacekeeper, willing and able to stand up to any Goliath.*

David made a very good companion for Sara from the start. I had wanted another child for precisely that reason—a playmate, friend, and confidant for my daughter, who was so bright and full of life—and by the time he was no more than two years old, David was fulfilling this role. Sara instantly recognized that in him she had the opportunity to practice her own precocious mothering skills. His maternal grandmother, too, fawned over him and spoiled him, constantly afraid when he walked or ran that he would fall.

This caused friction between Sara and David at first—Sara was accustomed to getting all the attention. But she was mature for a six-year-old. She handled the situation with grace, and she always loved her little brother. His easy smile and his ready laugh helped the situation as well.

There was always noise in the house in those days. Especially when David sneaked into Sara's room to take her things, as he sometimes did. This would invariably cause a fight. We would intervene and attempt to correct this behavior, but it did no good;

in his eyes, there was no such thing as private property for his sister. Still, he loved her. He was always eager for her to arrive home from school so they could play together.

When David was young, he loved to swim in the pool below our condominium apartment. He had a playgroup consisting of kids his age who lived in the condominium development. One of these kids in particular, Ben, became a close friend of David's, often coming over to our house and in turn inviting David over to his.

* * *

As David grew older, his creative and sensitive nature began to reveal itself. His favorite pastime was building with LEGO toys. He asked for them for Christmas, his birthday—virtually any gift-giving holiday. I was pleased this was his favorite. By that point I'd already recognized my son's affinity for fixing things, and I strongly felt that these simple toys offered him the chance to nourish that passion. Anything that encouraged his creativity was a winner in my book!

From LEGOs, he graduated to Transformer toys, which I also didn't mind. It was another plaything that I saw as a tool to spark his creativity. Between his grandmother and me, he never ran low on these toys he loved.

Other character traits that manifested themselves at an early age were David's sensitivity and compassion. One day when he was eight years old, I took our family to the beach. While we were there, I misplaced my sunglasses and had to look all over the beach for them. Sensing that I was anxious, David came over to help me look. At home that night, when we were about to say our prayers, David gave me a note telling me he was glad I'd found my sunglasses and that he loved me. In small but powerful acts such as these, he was always showing what a thoughtful soul he was. He displayed the same maturity of character in his interactions with both his parents and with his teachers and his friends.

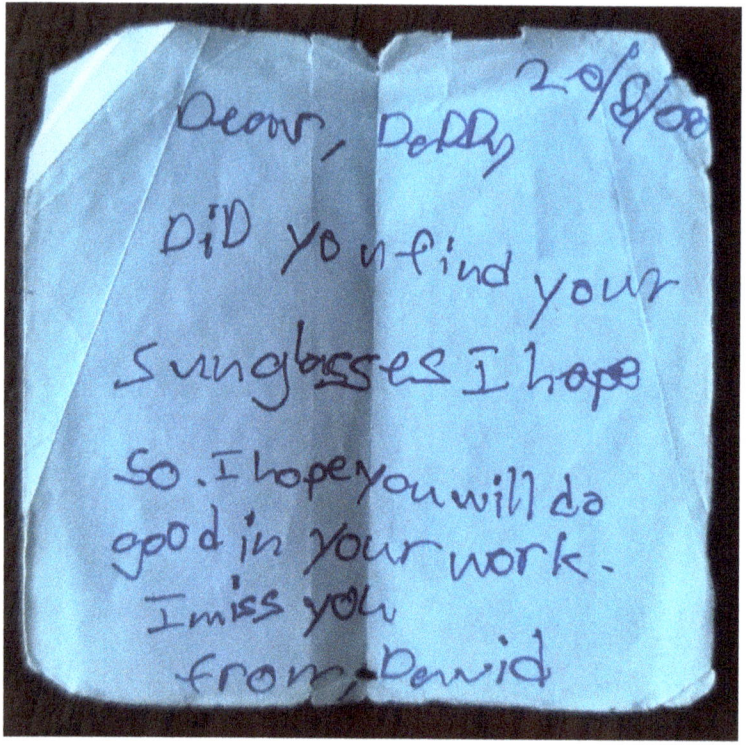

From the time David was in kindergarten until he was around twelve years old, during school holidays, he would go with me to the office. I would take the subway, leaving the car at home, and when we got to my office, he would work on his drawings or play with his toys. I would usually get done with work in two to three hours, and from there we would go to lunch or to the bookstore for some father-son bonding time.

Sara had a circle of friends her own age who also lived in the condo. She liked to play with them on school holidays, but David was different. He just wanted to follow me. When I went for business meetings, I would sometimes ask him if he wanted to come along, and he always did.

I had gone from working as an employee of Chevron/Texaco to running my own oil-shipping transportation business, and the thing I appreciated most about this change was the ability to set my own schedule so I could spend as much time as possible with my children. This luxury would prove indispensable when, at the age of nine, David's world came crashing down, and he needed support in a way he never had before.

* * *

I was the most important person in David's life, and we both came to depend on that closeness when Karen and I separated by mutual consent in 2006. I had custody of the kids, as Sara and David had made it known that they preferred to be with me. The challenges for the three of us from that point were daunting.

Sara and David were in grades seven and three, respectively, and it was a very difficult period of our lives. I was lost: Sara was showing signs of rebelliousness, while David wouldn't let me out of his sight. He was afraid of being left alone. I understood this and thus let him virtually be my shadow throughout this time period. But that still could not compensate for the feeling of abandonment he felt and the guilt that goes with it. David would be troubled by a fear of abandonment throughout the rest of his life. The difficulties faced by children who experience divorce can last a lifetime.

As a father, I was gripped by a sense of utter failure; I felt responsible for what had become of us. We had always prayed at bedtime, and we now did so with increased vigor. Sara led on many occasions, and her strength during this time helped keep what remained of our family unit glued together.

I made sure we all slept together in order to provide comfort and security to one another. On a few occasions, David, while fully asleep, would sit up on the bed in the middle of the night. I'd gently ease him back to a lying-down position. On one occasion, he got out of the bed. He walked out of the bedroom and down the hallway, calling, "Daddy ... Daddy." I woke with a start and rushed out to carefully guide him back to bed. After that I became a light sleeper.

I made an important decision: thereafter my children would receive my full attention, my full devotion. I spent fewer than four hours at the office each day and rushed home in the afternoon when the kids were done with school. The fact that I owned my business made it possible for me to focus more of my energies on the kids. Not that my shortened hours at the office didn't affect the business—they did. It just didn't bother me much.

I made an important decision: thereafter my children would receive my full attention, my full devotion.

Sara, David, and I set up a system of shared decision-making where the family was concerned. The children were empowered to think for themselves and to work through family issues as a team.

The three of us were very close, always doing things together—attending Mass every Sunday, going to their schools together in the mornings, eating dinners at home, watching TV together after dinner, and so on. We went to the movies together often. We took vacations to Thailand, Australia, New Zealand, Japan, Hong Kong, Bali, Korea, and Malaysia, among other destinations, and cruised from Macau to Vietnam and China. During our trip to Japan, we visited Universal Studios. We were having a fantastic time together, and I was feeling very grateful for my kids and the relationship we had. One of the shops we visited had a shelf of trophies. I bought one that read World's Greatest Son and gave it to David as a token of my appreciation.

I joined the parent-teacher association in Sara's school and attended the meetings. I also volunteered to help supervise Sara's and David's classes on their educational outings to museums and other historical sites. It was important for me to be actively involved in their lives.

Gradually the situation stabilized, and the children began to smile again. Sara, as the elder, was a very loving sister to David. She'd help him with his math homework, despite the fact that she had plenty of her own homework to keep up with. On many occasions, the kids went to bed past midnight because it would take that long to complete the day's homework—and then they had to be up at 6:30 a.m. for school.

I did the cooking, laundry, ironing, and other housecleaning. I fed and walked the dog. These tasks did not bother me in the least. The only thing that was difficult for me was seeing my kids in pain, and I made the choices I did in order to avoid that.

* * *

In 2008, two individuals entered our lives who would prove to be godsends. One was Agnes, a private tutor. She taught Sara initially, but it was David whom she would spend eight years with, tutoring him first in mathematics and later in Mandarin. They developed a special bond, and David was very fond of her. I never knew how much she loved and cared for him until he left us, and I saw how truly devastated she was. Agnes helped the kids develop a system of learning that proved invaluable to their intellectual development, and both kids became speed readers in due time.

Here, Agnes shares her memories of David.

Here is my version of David. Even before I taught him, I knew he was different. Creative beyond my comprehension. He would think of the most annoying prank to pull off on me and Sara: e.g. putting glue on the seat, turning off the lights when I was in the toilet, using my phone to text my friends. I almost quit! I'm glad I did not.

As he matured, got more involved in school, he became a determined young man. I remembered we once had tuition all the way till 11 pm, as he wanted to perfect his spelling, not that it counted towards his grades. It was just perfection he was after. No compromise, no flaws.

I remembered the day I saw the cuts on his arms and thighs. I was thinking of my approach as David was one sensitive and private soul. Though we fooled around and were more of friends, I knew that he rather I not mention it. Still I did. I had to. Subsequently, he opened up and shared his principles and philosophy. Hours and hours of it. I tried changing his mind but ended up being converted. He had that kind of persuasiveness. He exchanged his life to stand by his beliefs. Freedom. No compromise.

I believe he is at peace now.

During this same time, we hired our housekeeper, Edna, who had come to Singapore from the Philippines. I chose Edna because she was the first candidate who had that special chemistry with the children that I was looking for. Her previous professional experience caring for infants and toddlers transferred well to older children, and Sara and David took to her right away. Edna was just as fond of them. Here, she shares a bit of her experience watching David grow.

I started working for the Singh family in 2008. I remember that David was nine years old the first time we met. He was a very playful and adorable child. I used to cook breakfast for him and his sister, Sara. Every weekday, I made sure that they ate their breakfast and drank their milk before going to school. Before the school bus arrived, I helped David bring his stuff down to the waiting area. David's bag was huge and heavy—bags of primary pupils in Singapore are far different than way back in my home, the Philippines. It was like his bag was intended for a high school student.

David really loved shopping. He loved to buy toys and video games. One day, as I remember, we went to the mall with his father. I followed him wherever he went. As we were strolling around, he saw a toy he wanted. He asked his father if he could have it, but his father said "no." Then David got sad. His father really couldn't stand to see his son sad, so he agreed to get the toy. David ran to get it and I can't tell you how happy he was. We went back to the house, with David having a great time and full of happiness.

As time went by, David became a good teenager. The young man became tall, dark, and handsome. The little child who I used to help whenever he needed his bath suddenly became shy to me. *Well of course*, I thought, *he's a teenager now*. He became a bookworm also, finishing two or three books within a day.

One day, he received a letter containing the results of one of his university entrance exams. When he discovered that he passed, he jumped with joy like nobody was around. He was full of energy, asking me where his father was with overflowing excitement. His happiness overflowed like he won a really big prize in the lotto. Passing an entrance exam was indeed great news and we were so proud of him.

In Singapore, when a male child turns eighteen, they need to render their service to the army for at least two years. Nobody's exempt—every male child who turns eighteen is obliged to attend. David knew about it. One day, a letter from the military arrived at the house. It was for David. I gave it to him. He didn't open it, for he knew what it was all about. That's why he never opened that letter. Every time we talked about it, his mood suddenly shifted and immediately changed the topic. Until that nightmare happened. Even though he passed away, he's always in my precious memories, in my heart. I pray for him. I hope that in the next life we will meet again.

David's childhood before his mother and I divorced had been a happy one, and eventually, after we had worked together as a family to adjust, his life after the divorce was happy as well. While there were many bright spots in David's childhood, his early school years, unfortunately, were not among these.

* * *

The public school system in Singapore is elitist. At the end of third grade, children are segregated based on their performance on tests administered during the year. This means they are separated into lettered classes (A, B, C, etc.). Children from wealthy families get placed in higher-level classes because their families generally have the means to employ teachers privately to tutor their children after school and on weekends. Regurgitation is very much valued as opposed to critical thinking. David felt discouraged by this system, and he performed as no more than a middling student all the way through sixth grade.

Many children's spirits are crushed by this system, and unfortunately, there is no way around it. When you are a citizen of Singapore with a child in primary school, you do not have the alternative of private school—it simply isn't an option. You are not allowed to opt for private school until the child reaches thirteen years old. Before that, children are to receive a mandatory public-school education where their fears and anxieties are immeasurably heightened through a series of entrance examinations that are really designed to create a regimented and quiescent youth. To create a child or youth who does not question and instead does as they are told.

The Singaporean school system knowingly recruits parents as accomplices in piling pressure on the children. If a student has the misfortune to be merely average, their parents are called in. They are told by the school their child is falling behind, and they are strongly encouraged to press their child to study harder. There is no acknowledgment that children have their own pace for learning; if you haven't learned by eight years old exactly what Singapore thinks you should have learned, there's a problem.

Nothing crushes a child's confidence more effectively than an education system that puts a premium on uniformity and regurgitation of rote learning.

This suffocating system causes students to constantly worry about exams. Children don't get the opportunity to be children. Nothing crushes a child's confidence more effectively than an education system that puts a premium on uniformity and regurgitation of rote learning.

Additionally, the pressure to "excel" in order to compete for the limited number of spaces in the elite public schools is intense, and this breeds extreme anxiety among Singaporean schoolchildren. Many children in Singapore suffer from myriad psychological issues because of this system, which is designed to turn thinking children into docile workers. While our children achieve some of the highest ranks on standardized tests, the system takes its toll. In fact, the pressure spurred seventy-one students to take their lives between 2013 and 2016, the youngest of whom was just ten years old.[1]

Still, members of the government maintain a callous attitude, all but ignoring the mental and physical damage it does to children. "We want to retain a system that allows people to learn at their own pace but, at the same time, encourage more social mixing, empathy and programmes that allow students to do things together so they get to see each other for who they really are," Second Education Minister Indranee Raja said not long ago, glossing over the serious issues streaming continues to cause.[2] It is alarming but unfortunately not surprising.

The whole system capitalizes on the fear that is rampant in Singaporean society. It's the "fear of failure, fear of the government, fear of being shamed, fear of speaking our minds," as David's friend Liz explains, all of which is instilled in our children at such a young age. She remembers her parents telling her that she had to do well

---

1   Angela Jelita, "The Downsides to Singapore's Education System: Streaming, Stress and Suicides," *South China Morning Post*, September 21, 2017, https://www.scmp.com/lifestyle/families/article/2111822/downsides-singapores-education-system-streaming-stress-and.

2   Jolene Ang, "Streaming Still Has Role in School: Idranee," *The Straits Times*, November 2, 2018, https://www.straitstimes.com/singapore/education/streaming-still-has-role-in-school-indranee.

in primary school. If not, she wouldn't end up in a good secondary school, she wouldn't be able to find a job, and so on. As she so eloquently asks, "Are parents not meant to be the protectors of children, to encourage them to fail and try again, to be our safety nets, our pillars of support, and not the instigators of fear?"

David's friend Verena shared her memories of their time together after his passing, and her account captures some of the pressures—and corresponding struggles—children in Singapore experience.

> In grades 11 and 12, David and I connected more than before because of both of our psychological health issues. We both struggled with self-harm habits, and the fact that we could talk to each other about it helped us empathize and understand each other more. David began opening up to me more in his last few months. He would tell me about some of his childhood events that were hard to talk about. He also expressed his thoughts and views on how Singapore's authoritarianism, enforcement of the law, and governing of people affected him.

I knew how the school system worked, and I refused to give in to it; my children were just too important to me. Sara helped David when he struggled with math. I helped him with everything else he required, and we got through those early years together.

David was tuning out of the system. He was extremely individualistic, and the public education system does not reward thinkers and has little patience for them. The only thing David enjoyed then was Friday drama class at the Julia Gabriel Centre. There he could be himself. After his passing, the Julia Gabriel Centre published this powerful tribute to David:

A TRIBUTE TO DAVID SINGH

Two years ago, on 14th February 2016, a Julia Gabriel Centre (JGC) Speech and Drama alumnus sadly passed away shortly before enlisting for National Service. David Singh was an outstanding student who excelled in his academic studies at school; he completed his International Baccalaureate (IB) with a score of 44 and was contemplating studying Dramatic Writing or English Literature at university overseas. David was extremely creative and passionate about the arts. He wrote over 50 poems and a number of scripts, some of which earned him awards.

David attended Speech and Drama classes at Julia Gabriel Centre from 2006 to 2008. Under the artistic direction of Trevor Rodrigues, David's Speech and Drama teacher during that time, he showed great passion and interest in the arts. When he entered St Joseph's Institution International (SJII) High School in 2010, he enrolled in the Theatre Department to pursue this passion.

David's father, Harmohan Singh, told Let's Talk that he believes his son's love of drama blossomed while attending JGC's Speech and Drama classes.

"I like to think you helped plant the seeds for the drama class he attended in Primary (Grade) 4 and 5. One of this play scripts won 2nd prize in the national 24-hour playwriting competition in 2014 when he was 16 years old. David had intended to pursue Dramatic Writing in New York University. So, as you can see, it began with you and Julia Gabriel Centre."

If we played a small part in David's creativity and success, then of course that is encouraging. But, we believe that every child is an exceptional individual to start with and David, coupled with the unconditional love and support from his family, teachers and friends, proved in all areas of his life that he was an exceptional human being.

David is described by friends as having an analytical mind, a sharp wit, at times a twisted sense of humour. He had 'an effortless command for language,' notes David's friend Caroline. A passionate advocate for causes close to his heart, David often expressed his opinions and beliefs through his writing. The topics he wrote about cover subjects such as love, bullying, gender diversity, LGBTQ rights, and his views about the senselessness of war. Courageous and always authentic, David was not afraid to share his views about topics which are still deemed quite taboo in Singapore.

As a tribute to David, and in order to continue sharing his son's compassion and support for a variety of social issues, some of which he experienced first-hand, David's father, sister Sara and friends run a blog entitled Think to See (www.thinktosee.tumblr.com). 'Being yourself' was fundamentally important to David. he lived his life according to these values—he expressed his best self—and encouraged others to do the same.

You can read some of David's work on the blog set up by his father, who, in collaboration with family and friends, is currently working on a biography about David, due for release later this year.

At David's memorial service, one of his teachers from the Centre, Trevor Rodriguez, shared this message.

> I remember your smile, laughter, sniggering, and craziness during those speech and drama lessons at Julia Gabriel's Forum. You and the others certainly brought much laughter and joy to the lesson. Now it's your turn to create more laughter and craziness up there. Don't worry, God has a humorous side as well. Pray for us. We'll pray for you too.

As a team, Sara, David, and I discussed David's prospects. With help from my daughter, I convinced my son to enroll in a private international school in grade seven. It was in this new school setting that David's life changed for the better.

CHAPTER 3

David the Artist and Scholar

David was, first and foremost, an artist. While that term may be interpreted in a number of ways, to David, being an artist embodied freedom, peace, individualism, and the uncompromising pursuit of happiness through art.

At sixteen years old, David found himself increasingly drawn to theater, English literature, and philosophy; these intertwined

> *David was, first and foremost, an artist.*

interests led him to read voraciously on these subjects. In my parent-teacher meetings with Mrs. Pauline Bull, one of David's English teachers at St. Joseph's, I witnessed the strong bond between teacher and student and a lively rapport. In these meetings I saw that she truly understood my son.

If we, David's family, had entertained any doubt about the importance that literature held for him, or about the importance to him of Mrs. Bull, those doubts would have been assuaged by his will. David left some of the books from his beloved collection to this teacher who was so dear to him.

Similarly, there can be no doubt about David's importance to his English teacher, as evidenced by her words.

As a student of literature, David was probably one of the most intense individuals I ever worked with, and it was this love of literature, alongside his passion for theater, that led to our strong student–teacher relationship. David was also lucky to be part of a small class of higher-level literature students, and he enjoyed their support and their encouragement of his unique approach to the different texts we studied.

I remember, in particular, our study of Jane Austen's *Pride and Prejudice*, also Thomas Hardy's *Tess of the d'Urbervilles*. He knew I was passionate about Hardy's works, and after studying Hardy's poetry, David was keen to get on to the novels. We watched an excellent version of *Far From the Madding Crowd* to warm our appetites, and before long I found all in that class to be Hardy fans. When it came to *Tess*, David was deeply affected by Hardy's pessimistic attitude towards the society that denounced her as a fallen woman, and was most expressive of his condemnation of it.

On a lighter note, we came to school during the Easter break and watched the whole nine-hour BBC dramatization of *Tess*, stopping only for refreshments. By the end of the serialization the whole class was in tears, and deeply involved in the "virgin/whore" question—the debate over whether Tess was "a little whore who deserved her fate," or an innocent victim of an unforgiving society. David was particularly vocal in condemning Tess's fate and supporting her innocence.

On Teacher's Day, always a special day in school, David orchestrated a *Pride and Prejudice* party for me. They had turned some of the desks into a large dining table, covered it in a beautiful tablecloth procured from an unknowing parent, and David—without his father's knowledge I think—had brought in the best china tea set from home! While we ate scones and drank tea, each student chose one page from the novel and gave us their insight on the significance of it. It is the best lesson I have ever been involved with, and I believe it will take something special to beat it. (I'm also glad that your best china went home in one piece, Mr. Singh!)

As well as being David's teacher of English, I supervised his extended essay on *Equus*, in which he argued the case for science versus religion. The thing I remember most is David's enthusiasm for the project, and his independence in pursuing it. Indeed, I think I learned as much from David as I did from my own research of the play!

But my best memory of all is of the grade-twelve students' last day. Yes, it is prank day, but nothing bad ever happens, and this day was no exception. I came into my classroom to the most amazing sight. Somehow, David had borrowed two dummies from the drama department and, with the aid of the other literature students, had dressed them up as Mr. Darcy and Elizabeth Bennet to recreate their wedding. All the chairs had been set out for the guests, and we sat together while the students went through a mock performance. Bizarre, to say the least, but funny!

Most amusing of all, however, was a brand-new copy of the novel bought for me by the students and wrapped in paper that had been especially commissioned with my face replacing Elizabeth Bennet's! It was hilarious, and I still have it to this day.

---

* * *

In 2014, when he was sixteen, David participated in a national twenty-four-hour scriptwriting competition in Singapore. He was awarded the second-place prize for his script *Piety*, which touched on divorce and sexual identity. While these themes likely struck a chord with judges for their social relevance, they also bore great significance for David. He was able to transform some of his most daunting personal struggles into a work of art that earned him national acclaim. *Piety* has since been published in a compendium by Theatreworks (Vol 3, 2014–2015).

An adroit writer and more prolific than a lot of poets many years his senior, David left behind an impressive collection of poems, plays, and drawings, most of them created during the last twelve months of his life. These are his legacy. His poems in particular are indicative of the sensitivity of his soul and the idealism he fervently espoused. The following poem, "Leap," was among the writings in his black book.

LEAP

When papers fall like flowers in the empty sky

or parade across the evening gradient,

will you see freedom in all its fray,

or cages that bind conspicuous hope?

When colours march beyond the horizon,

effervescent Earth rises from slumber,

in more murky undergrowth in the misty morning,

will life charter forth a new course,

or banish into unfamiliar waters?

When love blooms innocently in hearts,
peace and serenity greet warmly,
kisses and hugs no longer yearn to be heard
Jealousy juxtaposed in destiny and fate.

If life gave you a chance,
A chance for a course to happiness,
to love.
Would you take it?

Of the many impressions his friend Liz can offer of him, some of the strongest involve his love of literature and his intelligence.

> David has an immense love for literature, and I'm sure we've all seen the way his eyes light up when talking about poems and books on war, individualism, existentialism, Marxism, and dystopian worlds. He gets more animated as he speaks, and his passion shines through. He's the friend who calls you up to ask you to read his poems, his plays, or just ask you random things. When David has passion or is interested in something, he researches everything about it and he remembers it all. That's probably why he's so intelligent.

To be David's close friend and confidant, according to Liz, is also to be his sounding board for his writing:

> I remember him texting me during his playwright competition, moaning to me about how difficult it was and how he was never going to win it. But guess what? He won it. Got second prize, I think. He constantly wrote poetry and plays. I remember the annoyance I felt when he interrupted me doing my homework and then threatened to end our friendship if I didn't proofread his extremely long plays and drama reports. I guess I never dared to tell him that it was truly an honor as his friend to be able to see him doing what he loved best, witnessing his stubbornness and passion for writing.

Exchanges such as these highlight just how headstrong David

could be. Along with being a tireless friend, creative mind, and precocious talent, David proved a stubborn advocate for whatever he deemed important. His demanding nature was an inextricable thread of his character—and it was not considered a fault by family or friends. This same unwillingness to budge made him an idealist and a staunch opponent to conscription.

> *His demanding nature was an inextricable thread of his character—and it was not considered a fault by family or friends.*

There's one of David's poems that particularly resonates with Liz, as he wrote it about her, three of their good friends, and himself on the occasion of their high school graduation.

FIVE

For Caroline, Katherine, Kimberly, and Liz; how we five hound the Sun. Happy graduation.

I
Now the burnt boughs stretch, their
Deadly nightshade oozes, seeps
Seeking through night's vacuum air—

How these hounds relish, burning
Like a sickle swing, head buckled,
For that carmine dawn, calling

In howling whispers to each
Branch of the sacred tether.
Nipped, Nyx's scions speak

Of their brutal births, twisted
Pacts carved in pelt, all savage
Under the new moon's blister.

We are the cysts of reverie
That burrow, arrow, grow—
Like flaming feral ghosts, close
To the New Apollo's vagary

II
And what of the fickle foils
The tools we left to dry, whose
Wings flicker and beat
Like fire laving in oil?

Those wintered bones I parted
To our delicate hands, twin

Stars, brooding, darted
To the nebulous eye
Staring, naked, at the fading coil?

Though our roads diverge now,
Thread thin and bare we quiver,
Shivering the haggard hoar
And reach, sweet sisters

As Bleached arrows
All cackles and calls
Running, yearning and burning
Even if any may fall.
—David Singh, November 2015[3]

David's friend Simren Sekhon gained a firsthand view of his theatrical abilities—a skill closely related to his love of literature—when the two acted together in the school musical *Oliver Twist* while they were in grade 7.

---

3   "Five" was initially published posthumously in *Infinitas*, SJII's alumni newsletter, for which we are grateful for the kind assistance of David's friend Madeleine and Ms. Ursula Ryan, advancement and communications manager at the school. The newsletter is issue 3, July 2016. The poem was published with kind permission of Caroline, Kat, Kimberly, and Liz.

David was the star of the show—he acted amazingly, sang wonderfully, and I still feel he stood out above all. I was lucky enough to act beside him as Mrs. Bedwin, a housekeeper, and I specifically remember a scene in which I had to stroke David's hair when I was taking care of Oliver Twist. David and I would always laugh [about] that ... and I feel privileged to have those memories with me now.

Kimberly, or Kimi, has generously shared many thoughts on her time with David—how he always impressed her with both his academic ambition and talent but also how valuable his friendship was to her.

When David and I were together we pretty much always had a good time, and if we didn't at least we bitched about it together. The biggest part of our friendship consisted of us eating together, and laughing, walking around aimlessly and just talking about anything. We were unhealthy food and non-exercising buddies together. We went to macs and shared secrets and struggles over hashbrowns and nuggets. We constantly gossiped and ranted like old ladies. We studied together, Tumblr-ed together, shared earphones and music and really weird inside jokes. We travelled together and took too many gross selfies and too little actual properly smiling photos. In New York, he once made me follow him to stalk this cute guy in a grey top for a good ten minutes in a museum; all the while pretending to just be looking for the "Starry Night" Van Gogh painting. It nearly happened another time in Ion's H&M, but the moment he saw the guy's shoes he was like never mind (they were Crocs). We would Skype and he'd link me to some funny video about some random thing like ducks or a model's falling compilation, and I'd say something not even close to the rudest thing he's ever said but he just would gasp and hang up ... and then call back like two seconds later like nothing happened. Or he'd just hang up randomly and then two hours later call me back and be like "Soz had dinner."

David is so creative, but sometimes I thought he used his talents for the stupidest of topics. He once sent me a fanfiction about Big Bird and Dumbledore, and even a love story he wrote about two lizards. We went shopping a lot too, and we'd give each other fashion advice. He'd make me try on the weirdest outfits in clothing stores and in return I helped him hide books he didn't think were good at the back of the shelves in Kinokuniya. He hid stuff everywhere actually, once we went shopping for heels, and I couldn't decide whether or not I wanted this pair from Zara, so he hid it in the men's section (which was pretty genius) so I would be able to buy it if I decided to later. Basically we were forever judging and insulting each other in the way only friends can.

He was really just his own person, which at times was truly shameless, and it makes me regret not saving my Snapchats of him at karaoke, or not remembering all of his funny comebacks because back then I was too busy trying to think of my own to follow up. I regret a lot of things when it comes to David, because he was more than just the friend that was hilariously rude in the funniest way. Because underneath all that sass David, is a really *really* good friend. He knew when I was joking and when I was genuinely upset, knew my insecurities without me having to voice them, went out of his way to include me and help me. I might not have confessed all my deep dark secrets to him like I did with others, but I think he somehow knew me just the same. He was the only person that really questioned my motives for wanting to pursue medicine, questioned my morals, my beliefs, because he was strong enough in his own ideals and principles that he could shake mine and break me out of ignorance I hadn't even been aware I was trapped in. I regret not trying hard enough to put myself in his perspective. He would go on and on in his complicated terminology about Marxism and existentialism and what freedom meant to him and I used to argue with him, and tell myself I could never fully believe what he did as we had completely different definitions of freedom. But now maybe I realise he'd already thought far beyond what my definition and its limitations entailed, because even though freedom is different to everybody, I think the kind of freedom David yearned for was too absolute for me to accept, or even comprehend at times, I hope it's the kind of freedom he enjoys now wherever his soul may be.

Thinking back on it now, I'm thankful, that I got the time I got with him, that he stayed long enough for us to make such happy and important memories. I know he tried very hard and that at times I must have made it harder. But I know he really cared about us, and about his future. He worked incredibly hard for IB, and when initially he didn't get his 7 for literature he was genuinely upset because he thought that meant Cambridge or

Oxford wouldn't accept him, and I sat with him and helped him research other US university options until he calmed down, and then when he remarked and did get his 7, I was happily expecting him to follow us to the UK. He had a plan for the future that we were all a part of, plans to travel everywhere, plans for endless hilarious karaoke sessions, plans for movies and board games—for me to finally be a doctor and for him to be there for me, for him to be an epic playwright and using his celebrity status to let me meet all my celebrity crushes. For him and I to plan Liz's bachelorette party together. I know that he cared for us in his own way. So I need to fight for him now, even though it's hard to even say his name sometimes. I need to stop being passive because that's what I was for most of our friendship, someone who would agree with him and go along with him and not argue back, not try hard enough to understand.

Another close friend, Caroline, shared her thoughts through David's tribute blog.

Dearest David,

I miss you deeply. It's hard to accept that two years have already passed since you leapt off this world into a new dimension. You have made a massive impact on my life, and I hope you knew that. You opened my mind. You, with your sharp wit, your deep analytical mind I could barely keep up with, your effortless command for language that often left me Googling words that tumbled out of your mouth, your searing passion for things that are important to you that made me start to think about my own values, and your twisted sense of humor that always made me laugh and know I had someone I could share a dark joke with. You never let anything fall below the standard you had set for yourself, often rolling your eyes or walking away from me if I said something that displeased you (after some verbal sparring). I miss your honesty. I miss your laugh. I miss your presence. "Only Love Can Hurt Like This, by Paloma Faith, was the last song you introduced me to, and is the one that always makes me think of you.

I tell myself, you don't mean a thing

And what we've got, got no hold on me

But when you're not there, I just crumble ...

... Only love, only love can hurt like this

... And every time, every time you go, it's like a knife that cuts right through my soul

Only love, only love can hurt like this.

David, your family loves you very much. Your father especially, David. You are so blessed. He is a great man I admire and love. Your friends love you too, even if we are quiet sometimes. It took me two years to work up the courage to write something on your blog, and I still think my prose isn't good enough, but this is from my heart to yours. I love you my friend.

Simren describes David's acting skills in *Oliver Twist*, saying, "I remember that he was also particularly good with accents—you name it, and he could do it."

David's sister, Sara, has this to say about his artistic and scholarly abilities—and how these were able to flourish at his school.

My brother was an incredibly talented young man—he could paint you a beautiful sunset, write you a poem, and star in a play, all in a day. It constantly amazed me, how gifted and brilliant he was. I still remember the first time I saw him perform. He was thirteen years old, and it was *Oliver Twist*. When he got on that stage and began singing, I was completely awestruck. Up until that point, I hadn't truly appreciated the magnitude of his talent. To see him stride across the stage with such confidence and passion, it just made me feel incredibly proud.

From then on, it was just all upwards for David. He fell in love with the theater, and constantly talked about musicals and playwriting. As someone who didn't have a creative bone in her body, I was amazed by my little brother and all the things that he was able to achieve.

While David's musical talent certainly included singing—crooning beautifully in school musicals and singing on karaoke outings—he was also skilled at the piano. David's piano teacher, Christina, shares the following about him.

I started teaching him to play the piano when he was fifteen years old. I was surprised initially that a boy his age would be interested to start learning music. I must say, my first impression was how rebellious and stubborn he was. Theory lessons were literally a battle of wills. He would just do a couple of questions per topic and then refuse to do any more exercises. No amount of cajoling or threatening could get him to do even one more exercise.

So I made a deal him. I'd test him to see if he understood—and he really impressed me! No matter how I twisted the question, he could still get the correct answer. It was at that moment that I accepted and trusted his judgment. He knew exactly what was enough. It was then I realized that this boy had his own agenda, and no matter what I did, I was not going to make him change his mind. He was an equal, not my student. Lessons went smoothly from then on.

Practical lessons were even more interesting. I would teach him a song and he would play it over and over and over again. For my other students, it's a chore to get them to repeat the song so that it gets better each time. In David's case, it was the opposite. He would play the song over a million times, till I begged him to stop. He was a true perfectionist! He learned to play songs like "Moon River," "Entertainer," "Blue Danube," etc. He played songs beautifully that were way above his supposed grade. It took a big effort to coax him to sit for the exam, as I knew he could ace it easily.

My son came into my room one day and told me he had to do a play in school called *The Coffin Is Too Big for the Hole*. It was his first literature project, and he thought the title sounded silly. That was where David's light absolutely shone through. His insights and explanations captivated my son and opened a whole new world to him. He was always fascinated with David's way of thinking. A boring play became filled with depth, full of controversy. He taught my son about soliloquies and other drama terminologies, and showed him a glimpse of an exciting world and a different way to interpret words. For that I'm truly grateful to David. I really miss the days when David walked into the room and the first words out of his mouth were "Hi, Peasant!" I know he's in a better place now, and I wish him well.

[Christina has explained that the nickname Peasant was a standing joke between them. One day when David showed up late for piano class, she greeted him by saying, "Hello, Your Highness." He replied, "Good day, Peasant." This banter became an ongoing part of their time together.]

David received adulation from other teachers as well—not just those who taught him literature, theater, and music. Many of them reported that his course research works were of a remarkable standard. I did not have the opportunity to fully witness this firsthand until one day in 2014, when David asked me to proofread his work on traditional Japanese theater. This was not a service he requested of me with any frequency, and I could not help but feel privileged that I was asked. The evening I sat down to read it, I discovered an astounding piece of work. I realized then that it was possible David was brilliant. Eventually I learned that his teachers thought so as well.

When David's aunt Sarge speaks of her nephew, she speaks of David's variegated artistic talent and his intellect. "My nephew David Cornelius Singh was a genius," she says. "He was an aspiring playwright, [and he] believed one should use to the fullest, the talents God has placed in him. He was a thinker and a well-read person. A brilliant scholar, he qualified to go to Cambridge, which was where he wanted to further his studies."

David was, in fact, deciding between Cambridge, where he wanted to study English literature, and New York University, where he would have majored in dramatic writing. He and I flew to New York in the summer of 2014 to vacation together with his friend Kimi and her parents. It was also to an opportunity for David to visit NYU again; it was his second visit to the city. The first came in 2012 when Sara, David, and I made a multicity visit to the United States, including NYC. During this visit, Sara accompanied David to NYU. She knew this was very important to him.

David had every reason to believe he would get into the school of his choice—in addition to proving a talented artist, he was also a strong student in every area he studied and was tested in.

David sat for his international baccalaureate in November 2015, scoring forty-four out of a possible forty-five points. He received distinctions in every subject he sat for, including Chinese Mandarin.

Liz noted that once David learned he could do well in a particular subject, he gained the confidence necessary to excel in areas he had previously found difficult: "I remember not really having to compete with him in chemistry in the beginning, but toward the last few tests, David and I were competing for first in class—proving that all he needed was encouragement and healthy competition!"

Simren also appreciates David's academic prowess, calling him one of her few friends who truly understood the SAT exams: "Both of us did them at the same time, and used to talk about questions together, and help one another with questions we didn't know. There was no one else I did that with."

While it is a commonly held belief that even a bright individual like David tends to demonstrate a strong aptitude in one suite of subjects at the expense of mastering others—being adept, for example, at literature and history but weaker in math and science—David demonstrated strong ability across the spectrum. Consider the following impressions shared by his math teacher, Sunanda Rao.

> "How could I make this silly error? Why did I not score 100 percent on this paper? So stupid of me." This was David speaking while we were revising for his grade-twelve mathematics examinations. He was intrinsically motivated to give his best in every area, be it mathematics or the languages or drama ... At the end of grade twelve, even when nominated as the best student for many subjects, David was so very humble and simple, which is a rare trait in seventeen-year-olds.

Sara nicely summarized what was so important about St. Joseph's Institution International in terms of David's artistic and intellectual development: "One of the places that my brother was able to be himself was at his school. It was at SJII that my brother developed into the vibrant and talented boy that we mourn today. For the first time in his life, David was able to express himself through the arts, and boy did he love it."

Addressing those who aided in her brother's growth as a confident, knowledgeable artist, Sara says, "I cannot thank his friends, teachers, and the administrators enough for making his time there such a joyful and fulfilling one."

CHAPTER 4

David the Young Man

David's teen years were loud and playful, filled with camaraderie, sarcasm, and wit. He was a lot of fun to be around. Take, for example the time when, one evening while I was asleep on my bed, he picked up the family's Chihuahua, Brundo, and laid the pet on my head. Early the next morning, I returned the favor.

Children can generally relate very well to animals—both are driven by love and innocence—and David and Brundo were no exception. They were inseparable at home. Brundo always sat by David's side in his study room.

In 2007, David said he wanted a cat. I was not sure if it was such a good idea since the dog might not appreciate it, but over the next few days, David kept pestering me for a cat—he was very good at that when he wanted something. Finally, we drove over to the SPCA to see if we could adopt one. David saw a lovely cat there, and I indicated to the staff that we'd like to adopt it. Unfortunately, the animal psychologist on staff wasn't so keen on the idea. When she learned that we already had a Chihuahua, she rejected our request.

Both David and I disagreed with her, but our protests fell on deaf ears. David left the SPCA fuming. Somehow, though, I knew this would not be the end of it.

The following afternoon, when I went to fetch him from school, he got right into it. "Let's buy a kitten!" I realized this discussion would continue until we satiated his passion. So I drove over to the same pet shop where we had gotten Brundo. We left the shop with a little ginger-colored kitten, whom David named Sally.

Sally, David, and Sara took to one another. Not surprisingly, Brundo took to Sally too. So much for the animal psychologist! Brundo and Sally would sleep side by side at times, and when we'd walk the dog in the evenings, Sally would tag along too.

Sally was a feral animal, as cats generally are. David was always concerned for her safety when she went outside. He wanted to lock her in his bedroom forever. While he knew that was not possible, he had the sense that the outside world was not safe for her. Two years later, Sally was run over by a car driven by a neighbor. Edna and I buried her under a grassy patch outside our home. Meanwhile, David was crushed, keeping to the confines of his bedroom for a long while.

One Sunday afternoon, just over a year after Sally's passing, I was having a cuppa at a McDonald's outlet near the coast. Suddenly, I heard "meow, meow." It was soft but clearly discernable. I looked around to locate the source. In the hedgerow just a few feet away was a tiny kitten. She appeared to be abandoned, looking somewhat malnourished. I thought for a few seconds, scooped her up, and called David. "Do you want a kitten?" I asked.

David didn't hesitate. "Bring her home!" he said. Over the next five years, the kitten grew to be a mummy, and from that single kitty, we amassed seventeen more. The house was a mess, including my furniture. Our neighbors were not amused either, especially with all the nighttime meowing.

The cats were a lot of work, but they also brought a lot of joy to our hearts. There was one occasion especially where David truly showed his devotion to his kittens. A three-day-old kitten in his litter had been abandoned by her mother. She looked sickly. David decided to do something about it. We went to the pet shop and got a feeding bottle and milk. Over the next few days, David fed the kitten round the clock. He would wake up before school to feed the kitten, later rushing home to check on her. Sadly the kitten did not make it. She took her last breath while David was at school. When I told David the news on the ride home, he was silent for the rest of the day. I can only imagine how he must have felt. For a child, a furry friend is a mirror image of himself—vulnerable, innocent, loving, and fun. To lose a friend is one of the most painful experiences he or she goes through. We go on to find new loves, new furry friends, but the memory of the ones that preceded them never fades.

Just as it was with his pets, David's teen years represented an era of—if not exactly figuring out who he was—making his thoughts, wishes, and personality known to those around him.

When he was sixteen years old, he came to my room and said that he wanted to talk to me. And I said, "Yeah, sure go ahead."

"Well, I thought you should know that I'm gay," he told me simply.

I looked at him, and all I could think of was, *How am I to protect him from discrimination and bullying?* Yet all I could manage to say to him at this critical time was, "Well, that's great. I'm glad you told me. We are your family, and we support you." I reached out and hugged my son. From the beginning, this was never an issue for me. I never viewed being gay as a *lifestyle choice* as some do; I saw only my son. I raised him, and this is who he is—a loving son, brother, friend, and human being.

The only concern I had is one I believe occurs to most loving parents upon hearing news of this nature: I worried about my son experiencing discrimination. It occurred to me that he might be bullied, that he might not be able to get a proper job when he graduated—this sort of thing. Some of these concerns were alleviated, however, when I saw David branching out at SJII, making friends with many students and also teachers, who clearly cherished and supported him.

One of these dear friends is Kat, who describes David in his teen years as being funny "both intentionally and unintentionally." She goes on to say, "He had an iconic laugh and an iconic sense of humor. He made every single moment so funny. He was also a very thoughtful friend. Every year, without fail, he would make me a birthday card filled with a bunch of memories that we shared between the both of us and with friends."

Having always been adventurous, David truly tapped into his exploratory side in his teen years, enjoying plenty of in-town adventures with his school friends but also taking exciting trips with them.

Kat fondly remembers two such trips—one to Laos during Challenge Week in their eleventh-grade year and the second to Hong Kong following graduation.

When I think about David on those trips, I remember just really bizarre inside jokes and small bursts of funny moments, like David helping us catch a cockroach in our room in Laos, or Kimi and Caroline making me and David watch a Chinese movie, and both of us just dissing the two main characters nonstop. Sometimes when me and Kimi get lost, we say to each other, "We need David here" because his sense of direction was so good …

I would say the memories that would stand out the most would be our trips together, including the sleepover where we argued and cried because I didn't understand his beliefs (but we made up after, so it was all good lol), all the times we went out with our friends and just had a blast, and finally all of our Skype calls where we would just basically be distracting each other for five hours and sending each other Buzzfeed quizzes to do.

His friend Liz similarly remembers many of the "small things" that made her friendship with David so special. She describes a reliable, loving friend who—at the same time—could be silly and petty. For instance, she recalls, "One moment he'd leave a WhatsApp chat group because he got angry and the next moment he'd privately text me begging me to add him back."

She additionally characterizes David as strong-willed and opinionated: "We've had loads of fights and arguments about religion, the government, and especially conscription in Singapore. We've literally gotten so worked up that we've thrown plates at each other in a restaurant."

Liz has been gracious enough to allow the inclusion of the memorial speech she gave at David's funeral, which appears here.

David's always been the friend that I hold dearly in my heart. The story of how we first officially became best friends is actually quite cliché. Usually, when you become good friends with someone, there's that awkward period in between when you're trying to decide if you're just a friend, or a best friend. David solved that awkward period really well. He gave me a keychain with the Hollywood star, with the letters BFF engraved in the centre. This pivotal event in our friendship was not just embarrassing for myself, but for David too. We never brought it up, but to this day, that keychain remains proudly hung on my pencil case.

David's the friend that does embarrassing things that never fail to make me laugh, and he pulls me into doing these deeds with him. Let me disclose a huge secret that David and I kept during IB. When he came over to my house, there were times where, instead of studying, we would watch *Totally Spies*, the children's cartoon show. We didn't just passively sit and watch it. No, we would stand up and mimic the character's actions. I'd play Sam; the brains of the group, the red haired girl wearing the green suit. David would insist on playing Clover; the bold and brassy shopaholic. This whole thing became our tradition, and it mortifies me to admit that we did this pretty frequently. Of course, the idea of seventeen-year-olds coming together to watch *Totally Spies* was something like our secret guilty pleasure.

Honestly, after being friends with David, your threshold for embarrassment is pretty high. We had a tradition where we would go for Karaoke and then eat dinner at Ichiban Boshi. David was exceptional at singing horribly when he wanted too, and also a really good dancer.

David's like the little devil that sits on my shoulder, whispering all the sassy comments and delivering sarcastic comebacks filled with big, bombastic words that always leave me confused. When David gets angry at someone, he's so funny and spiteful about it, it's truly hilarious. It's like he's on a warpath and no one dares get in his way.

He's very persistent as well, from the small things to the big issues. He comes over to my house and takes over my computer, playing songs that he wants me to like. And after the song finishes, he'll ask me, "Do you like it?" And if I say no, he makes me listen to it all over again until I like it. He also forced me to watch a seriously scary movie, *The Silence of the Lambs*. After the scene with Hannibal Lecter, the cannibalistic serial killer, he asked me: "Did you pay attention to the way the scene panned out? The camera action?" And obviously I did not because I was way too scared and freaked out. But David gave me no mercy and forced me to watch the scene all over again, pausing it to give his running commentary on how the camera angles reflected the power struggle between the police officer and Hannibal Lecter. Only David would subject his friends to this torture with the aim of making me analyze the scenes and characters. I am still quite scared of Hannibal Lecter.

David has an immense love for literature, and I'm sure we've all seen the way his eyes light up when talking about poems and books on war, individualism, existentialism, Marxism and dystopian worlds. He gets more animated as he speaks, and his passion shines through.

He's the friend that calls you up to ask you to read his poems, his plays, or just ask you random things. When David has passion or is interested in something, he researches non-stop about it and he remembers it all. That's probably why he's so intelligent. I remember having endless discussions with him on Marxism and Capitalism, freedom and equality, most of them occurring in our chemistry classes. These discussions could get pretty heated and after a while we would start getting personal and digress into insulting each other.

Ms. Okane, our chemistry teacher, would then be called over to our table because David would usually go, "Ms. Okane, Liz is being really mean to me." And knowing us really well, Ms. Okane would roll her eyes and reply, "Guys, you're like kids fighting in preschool. Do I need to call your parents?" And that usually shut us up.

Yet, I call them discussions and not arguments because while David and I occasionally don't see eye to eye on certain topics, he's always willing to push the discussion outwards and explore the points on both sides. But of course, he's refuses to change his beliefs and ideals. And that's what I admire most about him. Unlike the many of us teenagers, facing uncertainty and confusion for the future, unsure about ourselves as individuals or what roles we play in society, David knew exactly what he believed in and what he wanted to do. The depth to which he knew who he was is such a great reflection of how mature he is, compared to the rest of us. That's why he had the passion and guts to do whatever he wanted to do, regardless of anyone or anything.

I remember him texting me during his playwright competition, moaning to me about how difficult it was and how he's never going to win it. But guess what? He won it. Got second prize, I think. He constantly wrote poetry and plays amidst the IB course. I remember the annoyance I felt when he interrupted me when I was doing my homework and then threatened to end our friendship if I didn't proofread his extremely long plays and drama reports. I guess I never dared to tell him that it was truly an honor as his friend to be able to see him doing what he loved best, witnessing his stubbornness and passion for writing. The quality of writing that he produced was exceptional.

Right now, I miss David tremendously. Whatever I do, whenever I speak, or carry out any actions, I can't help but see that David has had such a great influence on me. Whenever I'm chatting to someone, it's like I'm waiting for David to interject with his sarcastic comments, flip his fluffy hair and give me his infamous eye rolls. His trench coat that he left in my house still hangs on my door. The books that he purposefully left in my house in hopes that I'd read it still lies on my shelf, not ready to be read. When the song "Hello" by Adele plays on the radio, I am brought back to our karaoke sessions where I can still hear David screaming obnoxiously during the chorus. When I read or watch something particularly interesting and stimulating, that's when I miss him most. I miss him being there, ready to listen, to explore and discuss new and old ideas.

I cannot stress how amazing a friend he has been, and how much he means to me.

I felt that Sara's speech during David's funeral was a true representation of what David was like, what he believed in, who David was, as a whole person. I know that my speech cannot be compared to hers, because she encapsulated what David believed in in three words. These unforgettable words are freedom, choice, and expression. I will always keep these values close to my heart, just as David did.

Some of the students David made friends with became close enough to regard him as family. For others the friendship may have been more casual, or confined to a certain context, but was still extremely valuable.

For instance, his friend Nicole, who is currently majoring in economics at Singapore Management University, shares the following.

I was fortunate enough to be in the same drama class as David during Grade 10. Although we weren't close, I was able to experience David's enthusiasm and contagious laughter during class. He was always very eager to learn new techniques and showcase his incredible talent to the rest of the class. I remember watching his monologue piece for our IGCSE [International General Certificate of Secondary Education, developed by the University of Cambridge] submission and the talent he had in acting was astonishing. The piece was so well delivered, emotionally touching, and real. He always brought life to our drama classes, as he always had this big smile on and always eager and ready to start class.

(After David's passing, I asked for and received from the school the audio of David's performance as described here by Nicole. She was not kidding—his performance truly was powerful.)

While Nicole does not remember all the details of the performance, she does recall with certainty it was a deep and serious rendition, which she believes was "an expression of his inner feelings." She describes an experience that has been common among those who witness David's acting firsthand: "I remember feeling impacted by his wonderful delivery. I felt that his piece made people reflect after watching his performance."

These friends of David's offer some of the richest available insight into who he really is, as they spent time with him across a wide assortment of situations. However, it is also true that David has the sort of effervescent personality with striking, precocious qualities that leaves a strong impression on family and friends of every stripe, along with adult acquaintances.

For instance, my friend Rick—someone I have known since we were college roommates in San Francisco—shares the following observation: "David was constantly engaged with Edna [our housekeeper] or his sister, usually giggling over some 'inside joke,' and he was clearly very affectionate with both of them. He also appeared to be a keen observer, with obvious intelligence."

David has the sort of effervescent personality with striking, precocious qualities that leaves a strong impression on family and friends of every stripe, along with adult acquaintances.

His sister, Sara, shares her unique insight into the rare qualities of independence, determination, and morality David displayed even from a very early point in life.

David was unapologetically David. He was someone who refused to compromise when it came to his values and beliefs. Many people spend their teenage years trying to search for who they are—I certainly spent a long time struggling to find myself. But with David, there was no struggle. He knew what kind of individual he was and what kind of life he wanted to lead, and there was no person, or construct or institution, that could stop him from becoming the person he wanted to be.

See for David, life and living was always about freedom, and choice, and expression. Those were the things he valued right until the very end. In fact, he once wrote a collection of poems that he said were "meant to sustain voice in a world that constantly attempts to stifle it." Quite honestly, I can't think of anyone who was more sincere and authentic than my little brother. If there was ever a person who was able to "sustain his voice in the world," that was David …

At home, David was also a master of achievements—he was a beloved son, brother, grandson, nephew, and cousin. He just had this way of lighting people up with his unstoppable wit and quick humor. In fact, we used to just sit in front of the television for hours laughing at the most ridiculous things. It's almost impossible to put into words how much my brother meant to everyone in my family:

- For my parents, my brother was the biggest bundle of joy they had ever received, and I know that every moment they spent raising and loving him was filled with immeasurable delight and gladness. My brother was a star in their eyes, and they were immensely proud of all the things that David was able to achieve and of the person that he had grown to become.

- For my grandparents, David was the most darling and precious grandson that they had. As a kid, David used to always look forward to Wednesdays, because that was the day that my grandparents would visit our home. He used to spend hours playing games with our grandma and was also a big fan of my grandpa's wonderful cooking. I know that those moments he shared with my grandparents meant a lot to him because he loved them very much.
- For my aunts and uncles, David was always a bright and vivacious young boy who brought them great pride and happiness. He was a unique young man who had his own special identity. He was both a joy and a mystery, and I know that my aunts and uncles will dearly miss him.
- For my cousins, David was a vibrant character who brought them much delight. I know that the countless hours that my cousins spent playing with David when we were all kids will form a memory that they will treasure forever.
- For my housekeeper, Edna, David was the little boy she never had. She spent many years with my brother and was incredibly close to him. The times that they spent playing and laughing together are moments that she will never forget.

Two years after his death, Sara shared the following message.

Simren, his good friend since grade seven, has many fond memories of David, whom she considers one of her first true friends from SJII. She tells of meeting David in seventh grade, when the two shared a tutor group and also happened to sit side by side in music class for lessons in Gamelan—a type of ensemble music, heavily reliant on percussion, which derives from Java and Bali in Indonesia.

In him, I found someone who was extremely easy to talk to, humorous, and jovial—in him I had found a friend of six years.

Another vivid memory I have of David was at my birthday party that same year—I especially remember Zylphia, a classmate of ours, chasing him around the pool and in return, David's piercing scream as he ran away.

Truly, David had no qualms about being who he was, in all sincerity. When he had invited me for his birthday, above being there for David, I remember sitting and talking to Uncle Mohan for a while—I was able to better understand the man who I had seen was always there for David in school, no matter what was happening ...

Another quality of his that was really inspiring to me was his dedication. Take athletics for example. He used to hate going for it, and truth be told, I used to cheekily tease him about doing it, but I now see that the fact he stayed on for the time that he did in the activity was representative of his determination. I think this was especially so in Model UN—the sarcastic, funny David I knew was so good at composing himself and speaking like the intellectual that he was. The range of talents that he has never ceases to inspire me.

When I think about David now, there are two standout memories for me. The first was for my birthday party in grade ten—he came with balloons, and not birthday balloons but baby shower balloons, saying things like "Congrats! It's a girl!" I'm sure everyone else at the restaurant was somewhat bewildered at why there was a baby shower on a table full of teenagers, but regardless, it was a good laugh. The packaging of his birthday present is the one I've still kept till today—it was a gold box with a collage of Hrithik Roshan, my favorite Bollywood actor, who David used to love to make fun of me for liking. His creativity never ceased to bring a smile to all of our faces.

The second memory that remains clear to me is on the last day of grade twelve. David was sitting two seats to my left and when it was announced that I had won the "Josephian of the Year Award," I remember looking at him before I went up to collect the award.

Here Simren conveys a scene that truly summarizes the type of friend David believes in being. "He was screaming, cheering me on and clapping," Simren reports, "and I think that it's really rare to find a friend so genuinely supportive and happy for me."

While it has been natural for us—David's family and friends—to focus on what we have lost in the time since David left us, he provides us a wealth of beautiful memories to concentrate on as well. When Simren thinks of that day David cheered as she proceeded up to claim her award, she says, "That is the face that comes to mind whenever someone speaks of David now."

CHAPTER 5

David's Politics, Philosophy, and Spirituality

David wrote a haunting dedication for the collection of poetry he left behind, which he titled *Fool (Or the Twenty-Five Times I Killed Myself)*.

FOOL
(Or the Twenty-Five Times I Killed Myself)

Ours has been a history of war.
This is for the countless who
Refuse to let our future be so.

Below it was an excerpt from the poem "Suicide in the Trenches," by Siegfried Sassoon:

> You smug-faced crowds with kindling eye
> Who cheer when soldier lads march by,
> Sneak home and pray you'll never know
> The hell where youth and laughter go.

At a tender age, David was already tackling some of the social issues that perennially make news headlines: LGBTQIA rights, gender equality, feminism, and social inequality. He also believed in existentialism, in the value of personal choice, and the power of free will.

> *At a tender age, David was already tackling some of the social issues that perennially make news headlines: LGBTQIA rights, gender equality, feminism, and social inequality.*

When he was in twelfth grade, he insisted that I read *The Stranger*, by Albert Camus. I was preoccupied by my daily chores, and it took me some time to get to it. After a week, David became antsy, pestering me on a daily basis to get down to it. It was obvious that he found the book and the story of innate interest and wanted to share it with me. Or was there something more to it? He threatened to take back the book if I delayed reading it any longer.

It was classic David—passionate about his interests and just as committed to sharing them. In the book, Meursault, the protagonist, is dedicated to pursuing his own freedom, in spite of not only his circumstances (his impending execution), but also societal norms and restrictions. Both Meursault's and David's lives reflected Camus's assertion: "The only way to deal with an unfree world is to become so absolutely free that your very existence is an act of rebellion."[4]

Camus was undoubtedly an influential thinker, essayist, novelist,

---

4 Albert Camus, *The Rebel: An Essay on Man in Revolt* (New York: Knopf, 1956).

and playwright. I would venture to say that he was arguably the most resolute and unapologetic practitioner of his craft. He believed in himself, in the primacy of the individual—just like David did. Camus was many things to many people. To scholars, he was a Marxist, a surrealist, existentialist, dramatist, absurdist, nihilist, syndicalist, federalist, anarchist, and more. To David, he was a pacifist—a compassionate human being who inspired him through his words and his deeds. [5,6]

As I have emphasized from the beginning, my son was a conscientious objector; he, too, was a pacifist. His commitment to peace, egalitarianism, and individual liberty did not waver even in the most intimidating of circumstances: military conscription or what is commonly termed National Service in Singapore.

As I have emphasized from the beginning, my son was a conscientious objector; he, too, was a pacifist.

David took his life rather than become part of any vehicle for war or violence. He hoped through his sacrifice to raise the issue of the stupidity of war and military service, which he felt ultimately served only those in positions of authority while demanding deep sacrifices—physical and moral—from those who serve.

He hoped by his untimely passing to raise awareness against National Service and war, so that hopefully future generations of young men would not have to serve and be sacrificed. He wanted to

---

5   Cory Massimino, "Albert Camus's Common-Sense Case for Pacifism," The Circle Molinari, May 16, 2015, https://thecirclemolinari.com/2015/05/16/albert-camuss-common-sense-case-for-pacifism/.

6   David P. Barash, "Neither Victims Nor Executioners," *Psychology Today*, November 7, 2013, https://t/www.psychologytoday.com/us/blog/pura-vida/201311/neither-victims-nor-executioners.

help restore these young men's opportunities to live their youthful dreams.

It is evident that my son considered military conscription an evil worth protesting with his very life, and while I would do anything to bring him back and support him in realizing his noble ambitions here in this life, I have nothing but respect for his uncompromising adherence to his values. I can see clearly that David's rejection of National Service was no isolated political stance—he did not regard conscription in a vacuum.

David understood conscription for what it is: the harshest sort of indoctrination of Singaporean nationalism. In the same vein, David obviously saw through this cardboard notion of national pride. He saw—at a precocious age—that to succumb to this was to be brainwashed, to accept that you were what the government considered you: a number, a pawn, a weapon when needed for war—but less than a person in peacetime.

My son's resistance against conscription arose naturally from a full suite of beliefs he held dear. For him, conscription may have represented a noose, but the government had built the gallows with a thousand slights to individual rights and human dignity.

While David was a compassionate soul from the time he was quite young, in high school his worldview burgeoned into a more sophisticated belief system. David's close friends witnessed the evolution of his philosophy and politics on a day-to-day basis. In the time after his passing, these friends testified on numerous occasions to the strength of his character—how he dedicated himself totally to whatever pursuit he found worthy, how he stuck to his convictions, no matter whether they were popular. Here I include accounts from two of my son's dearest friends on the nature of some of those convictions.

> David's close friend Kat shares the following about him.

David was one of those friends who'd correct you (in the sassiest way) if you said something politically incorrect, even though in grade 10 I wouldn't have known better. David was the friend who would proudly say, "I'm feminist," to a group of clueless high schoolers who could barely grasp the concept, way before people thought it was cool to write that they were feminist in their Instagram bio. Back when everyone cared so much about appearances and how other people perceived them, David was truly himself in every way possible. And he knew we loved him for who he was.

David had very controversial opinions, but he stuck to all of them and tried to get us to understand his point of view, no matter how frustrating we got. Looking back, he was probably thinking that we were a bunch of dumb-asses because none of us were as "woke" as him. It took all of us forever to understand why he was Marxist Existentialist, why he hated the government, why he hated the military. He was defiant and stubborn and stuck to what he believed in till the very end.

One of the last times I saw David was at a sleepover, and we got into a huge argument because he said he would rather die than go into the military. We were both crying so much, I'd never seen David so upset before. I didn't understand why he would die for his beliefs, and I genuinely thought he was being selfish. We made a pact that he would go to prison instead of joining the army. The more we talked about it, the more I understood his point of view.

> I knew he was getting help from a therapist, and I guess I felt stuck and didn't know what else to do. I felt like all I could do was listen to him and love him for the way he was. I couldn't have changed his beliefs no matter how hard I tried. I don't really know how to say it, but nothing in this world could have changed the way he was.
>
> Everyone else around him was growing and changing, conforming to social norms, being completely unaware of all the political and social injustices that happened in the world, and David was the only person whose eyes were truly open to everything. David's dad once said that he knows David is an old soul, and I know it too. David was wise, he was brave, he was intellectual and creative. I admire him so much. He'd do all of this without seeming one bit pretentious. You knew from the bottom of your heart that he was genuine. I regret that I didn't learn more from him in the time we had together.

Even as my son's specific politics and philosophy ripened with his maturity, he never shifted away from his core principle of standing up for what was right—for everyone. His friends have attested to the fact that he did not back down, nor did he wait for a position to become trendy before publicly supporting it.

There are countless traits I admire about my son: his fealty to who he was inside, his wit, his intelligence, and his perseverance. But there is no quality of his that I revere more than his bravery. When David Cornelius Singh believed something was right, he refused to hide his objections from anyone. He spoke openly to his friends and family about his beliefs, and he did not hide them when menacing authority was bearing down on him. My son could not have made his opinions about Singaporean politics and culture any plainer.

While he expressed his views through actions and deeds, his go-to means of expression was always his writing. In his plays and in his poems, David conveys the depth of his feeling against the corrupt Singaporean system. Because he expressed himself so eloquently, and because it was his wish that his message be heard loud and clear, I include his own writing here. As usual, it is David who says it best.

WAR GAMES

"I see the boys of summer in their ruin
Lay the gold tithings barren
Setting no store by harvest, freeze the soils"
—Dylan Thomas, "I See the Boys of Summer"

Echoes spark spirals, pinning hope down—
Then I awake to hauntings of gargled flesh
Gaping gashes like mouths that drown on
Blood congealed in mounds of trash;

Where you pool, glimmering ghoul
Cheshire grin on your harlequin tool
Who do you think you are,
On your sickled pulpit, great lampoon?

Cowardly murderer
Like a mindless maggot you
Spurn hot spit on us, the scavengers.
Writhing worthless as worms, whose

Fault led us to the slaughtering croon
Of the blackest hour only midnight blooms.
That sweeping sorrow I drowned in
To now awaken with a hideous smirk:

Fickle fiend, you thieve our souls.
But your soul was long lost, like ash
That incense you burned in turn for your rule;
They feed on you. You dirty dim tool.

There is a long poem David wrote, titled "Touch Me," which he left for me along with the rest of his writing, depicting his evaluation by the military psychiatrists. Sections of that poem are sampled elsewhere in this book, but I would like to include another section here, which again underlines how deeply and personally David felt the effects of this system. He makes it clear in these words to what he ascribes the endless violence and loss of freedom accompanying conscription:

Crushing our freedom so the carnage
Seeps into evenly cracked nooks

Of piles of money in piles of bodies
Of valor and bravery
To scare their "enemy"
So their pride stays intact and un-smothered in the cradle
So they can tell you that war is a necessary evil
So Mr. Prime Minister can change your troubles
Crush the future of burning fools
Stuck in chains to this country's stools

For fucks sake just let me go

You do not need me you do not need us

You have enough, don't wrap us whole

In his adolescent years—a time of life when many of us tend to be dramatic, self-involved, and vapid—my son was dissecting the so-called patriotism he'd been surrounded by his whole life. He was taking it upon himself to look beyond the facade to discover what true and ugly motives thrummed in the heart of this all-encompassing national pride.

As I read over his writing, I see him vividly yet again. I see his sharp mind paired with his empathetic heart. These qualities made David the individual he always was: someone who believed in fair treatment, honesty, and freedom for everyone, from the highest-regarded government official to the forgotten underdogs of society. His writing makes it apparent that he understood the greed at the root of Singapore's many social ills. He understood that this greed extended beyond the government's habit of bleeding its citizens and wooing foreigners at any cost in order to shore up the coffers. David realized that this greed was more than monetary—it extended to a voracious hunger for human life itself.

It was not enough to beat into the minds of impressionable youth that Singapore was the best nation on earth, deserving of their loyalty, their greatest chance for a bright future. It was not enough to use the citizenry to maintain government cash flow while promising these citizens a better future that would never come. The government continued taking life after life under the banner of conscription.

My son said it plainly—"You have enough"—and this is true.

How terrible it must have been for him to understand that the military was a fully staffed institution already, that there was no current threat against which Singapore needed defending, and yet that he would be forced to participate in it. Because of national duty. Because it's what's done.

> *My son said it plainly—"You have enough"—and this is true.*

In his poem, David calls out the military's (and therefore the government's) false interpretations of "valor and bravery"—notions used to guilt the public into supporting corrupt practices. The Singaporean government has no comprehension of, nor claim on, these words. In his firm opposition—in his fidelity to his own insistent point of view—my son embodied the true spirit of them. David is the one who represents valor and bravery.

I would like to end this chapter with more from David's dear friend Kimi. Her words about my son's politics and vigorous integrity are a perfect summation of who David is.

> He directly told me he wanted to kill himself one time. It was one of the first times I was drunk. We'd just received our IB results and had taken shots in Liz's house. The three of us had ordered McDonald's delivery to celebrate. When the delivery man came, David and I answered the door–he was the less sober of the two, so I dealt with the money and told him to check the order. The delivery man left with a typical "Thank you. Have a nice day." To which David had yelled back, "She just got a 44 for IB. Of course she's having a nice day!" Or something like that. Like I said, we were sloshed at this point, and the main thing I remembered was his saltiness at both me and Liz beating him in IB by one point

(he'd only later get a remark that raised his grade from a 43 to a 44). I'm not quite sure what he and I discussed in between then and all of us going back to the bedroom, except it involved helping Liz throw up, and stealing her nail polish to paint her nails horribly whilst she was knocked out from the alcohol. It was in the bedroom where he'd said something along the lines of how he would rather die than be enlisted. I was tipsy, and at a loss for words, I desperately wanted Liz to be awake because I didn't know what to say.

"Don't," I definitely said. "Don't do it, there are other things you can do to fight." I think that was literally the strongest defense I could come up with. He said he'd do it with a rope and hang himself on his fan. That he'd Googled stuff. I had no idea how serious he was being. Every day people jokingly throw phrases around like "kill me now," or "I swear to god I'm going to kill myself." We threw those kind of phrases around, but this was definitely different. I didn't know it yet, or I denied it, telling myself he wouldn't actually do it.

We later went for karaoke and had sushi and that day we had together remains as one of the fondest memories I've ever had with him. I never brought it up again, and neither did he. I was relieved because I wouldn't have known what to say, I didn't want that responsibility. I was very selfish and scared and it was easier to not confront him. I did nothing. I knew he was taking medication. I knew how much he hated NS—National Service—and conscription. But we had so many other happy moments together, other lunches, other karaokes, whole trips to Laos and Hong Kong together. We even had lunch on the 13th of February—a Saturday—with Liz. It was the day before he would die, and I don't know if he even knew it then. He seemed completely normal. We talked about meeting up the next day because we were both salty singles and it was Valentine's. He offered to bake at his place and I said no because he lived so far away. I didn't text him after that, partly because there was a part of me that was dreading the NS talk I knew was coming when he would enlist and also because he had already agreed to meet me on my birthday, which was the following Friday. At Saturday's lunch he said he would book out by 5pm so I arranged to go bowling in the evening. I let myself forget that drunken moment until the phone call came telling me he died. Then I couldn't stop picturing him hanging from a fan. I couldn't even bring myself to ask his father how he died because I was so scared of the answer.

Here's the thing about David though: he is *so* brave. Braver than I ever could have been. You know the feeling when someone pisses you off? Like when a teacher is rude to you and makes you angry and after class you rant to all your friends about it, and they tell you what a horrible person this teacher must be and it makes you feel better. You might even make up something witty that you should have said back to their face, and your friends would agree and suggest something else you could have said and suggestions would pile until you had a whole speech prepared to throw in said teacher's face. Then you'd laugh it off and go back to life. Very few of us would actually even think of talking back to the teacher. Never be brave enough to face the consequences. Especially when brought up in a country like Singapore, where rules are gold, where grades and thus by extension a teacher's opinion of you meant more than it ever really should, where rebellion is so widely rejected.

David on the other hand has no such qualms. After he received his IB results, he sent an incredibly sarcastic, sassy email to one of his teachers who he felt had had no faith in him, "thanking" her for all her help whilst really just saying "I got this grade all on my own thanks for nothing." He'd talked about it but I was actually shocked he actually sent it and cheered when he read me the message over Skype thinking "Wow I could never do that." Although not condoning being rude to teachers I'm just trying to say he was never afraid to stand up for himself if he felt he was in the right and he urged his friends to be the same.

When he wanted to see *The Danish Girl* in cinema, and I told him we were too young and they might not let us in, he demanded we try anyways, demanded we go up to the counter and ask why this movie was rated R21. Why we were too young for the non-conservative, nontraditional message this movie was about. I rolled my eyes in response. The people working wouldn't care about that. They'd just be all "I'm just following the rules" or "Sorry, my boss says no." At the time I didn't see how special this made him. Where most people would blindly accept and follow, he questioned and even when most would find the answer acceptable he'd question it more until he received an answer he could accept.

Why do boys in Singapore have to serve national service?

Oh, because it's the law there, everyone has to.

But why?

Because Singapore is small, so all the boys have to go or there won't be enough people.

But why?

Because a country needs a military.

But *why*?

Because we have to protect ourselves, the boys give up two years of their freedom, for the freedom of the rest of the nation, for the freedom of the rest of their lives. Freedom to live without fear of violence looming over our shoulder like other countries did. Freedom to be educated, to work, freedom to receive all the many benefits Singaporeans do. There is a lot to be grateful for as a Singaporean and we have the national service amongst other things to thank for that.

This had been the answer I'd accepted. That I think much of the country would agree with. That complete freedom although ideal was impossible in life, that some form of sacrifice had to be made. We once had a really bad argument about this in school, where I told him you couldn't satisfy everyone in the world. It was impossible. So obviously you had to try to satisfy at least the majority. "Even if that meant the minority suffers?" he'd questioned. At a defeat, I realised and replied, "Yes." To that he had said, "People like you are the reason I want to kill myself."

After that, the bell rang and he went to class. I sat on the bench in school and tried not to cry. It's now too late for tears because I swear it was so hard to see at that point in time but it became so crystal clear the moment after I was told he had died.

It's like this. The problem about David's absolute freedom is that I was right in a sense. It is largely impossible in the world we live in. I can talk all day about how I hate the Singapore military, but someone will always be able to argue against me; repeating what I already know. I can understand why people would think it is a necessity. Many might even say they're grateful for NS, it helped them mature, grow, become a better person etc. ... But none of that is the point David had tried to make me see.

Singaporeans have largely just accepted it. There are people who support NS, there are arguably more people who hate it—people like my brother, like many of my male Singaporean friends that will just say, "I'm glad it's over, I hated it." But you can hate something and accept it at the same time. Very few are like David who actively fought against it. What David wants, this absolute freedom as I coined it in my head seemed so far away in the future (if even possible in the future)—generations and centuries away from the world we're in. It's such an ideal, almost dystopian concept that people don't even take it seriously. The ways we're stuck in—conscription—seems logical. Not ideal but logical. So it is accepted.

The point is that conscription is making people do something against their free will. Conscription is the opposite of freedom. With conscription people are not free.

I was once taught that morality is an individual's perception of whether something is good or bad, ethics is a group of people's idea of whether something is right or wrong and legality is a government's law on whether something is legal or illegal. Well then, I believe conscription is bad, and many will agree with me when I say it is wrong and should be illegal. But it isn't.

To me it is so clear. It should not be done. The rest of it—the logistics, the necessity of it—is all background noise. Obviously no one can wave a magic wand and get rid of conscription, but it is a fact that should be more acknowledged. Instead of people just complaining about it and not doing anything, they should be acknowledging that it is an issue and pursuing or even just considering other options. But it's not. When people just blink and say it can't be done and move on it's so frustrating to me because David's death has just made it black and white. To me it's like someone in the past who probably thought, "Yeah of course I *need* slaves, who else is going to build my house and harvest my crops?" This might sound extreme, but it *is* extreme to me the way it was extreme to him.

The Singapore military has caused the death of my friend. They threatened his freedom—after hearing him say it was something so important to him that he would rather die than live without, and so they forced him to take his life. Yet people still go around saying things like, "Yeah, but we need NS." They are saying my friend's freedom *needed* to be taken away. My friend *needed* to die.

It hurts me because I was once one of those ignorant people.

Lots of people throw around the phrase, "If you don't do this/If this doesn't happen, I swear to god I'm going to kill myself" but they never really have what it takes to follow through. David did.

He refuses to have his freedom taken away from him. He refuses and it shows me how wrong conscription is.

And as much as I want him here, as much as I still whole-heartedly believe everything could have gone so much better, I have to admit how much his death taught me. I just wish I could have understood it faster, supported him better.

David hadn't been satisfied with my answer and now neither am I, neither should you.

It's really hard. I tell myself I need to fight, I need to get this message out, because he fucking died trying to get this message across to us and so this message can't die with us. It's hard because it's been ingrained in most Singaporeans that NS is the way it works, and I know firsthand how hard it is to snap out of that mindset, to step back from the whole "necessity" of it to first accept this is not a good thing and that action should be taken. The first words to that are always "but what else can you do?" to which I can't even answer because I don't know, but it's beside the point. Conscription is wrong the way slavery is wrong, the way women not being able to vote is wrong, the way being racist or sexist or homophobic is wrong. It doesn't matter that there isn't a clear solution for it yet, it just shouldn't be accepted.

It's hard because when I tell people, they can't see past the clinical depression. "Oh, he was depressed," they say and they accept that as the answer. It's not. It's so much more than that. He was forced into a situation that was wrong and it was like only he saw how wrong it was. It must have been isolating.

There is a lot of guilt and regret because I was part of that process that isolated him. Because he confided in me and I should have done a lot more.

He has definitely changed my life and I miss him every day.

CHAPTER 6

David's Depression and Psychiatry in Singapore

On my deathbed I will pray
To the gods and the angels
Like a pagan to anyone
Who will take me to heaven
To a place I recall
I was there so long ago
The sky was bruised
The wine was bled
And there you led me on.
—from "Like a Stone," Chris Cornell[7]

I heard this song before realizing that the singer, Chris Cornell, had a history relevant to David's story. A brilliant musician, songwriter, and poet, Cornell sold more than fourteen million albums in the

---

[7] Audioslave, *Like a Stone* (California: Epic, 2002) www.chriscornell.com.

United States, and more than thirty million worldwide. And not so long ago, after suffering a long time from depression, he took his life.

This hits close to home for me, of course, because my dear son, David, took his own life after suffering from depression as well. At eighteen, he refused to be drafted for military service in Singapore. Ten years earlier, he had first informed me he was never going to allow himself to be drafted. I was surprised by his words. He was so young and tender ... and yet he knew. The Singaporean government, however, does not recognize conscientious objection. It's either be drafted or go to jail—and then be drafted anyway.

> *The Singaporean government, however, does not recognize conscientious objection. It's either be drafted or go to jail—and then be drafted anyway.*

David said he was prepared to give his life so that other youth need not be forcibly conscripted into military service against their religious and spiritual beliefs. In him one could see evidence of a civic mindset and character rarely embodied in today's world: a true pacifist.

A pacifist is the deepest manifestation of our humanity. We may think we have strong religious convictions, yet we find ways to justify our advocacy of war and violence. But violence is not consistent with the teachings of Jesus, Buddha, Gandhi, Martin Luther King Jr., or Henry David Thoreau—the man who inspired Gandhi and MLK. David understood this better than most of us, including me, his father.

A misinformed person said to me soon after David's passing that there was no such thing as a conscientious objector in Singapore. Even though this person was a relative, it was instantly clear to me that he did not really know my son. Two days before he was to report for military service, David gave his life as a final act of civil disobedience. The state had rejected his pleas based on his religious beliefs as a pacifist and conscientious objector.

The state also rejected a plain and valid reason that David should not have been conscripted: he was suffering from depression. In my son's case, the depression itself arose from his anxiety about being conscripted. This was recognized by a psychiatrist; David had been diagnosed with clinical depression. And yet he was forced into military service—the known cause of his depression.

David's basic human rights were denied to him. His dream was to pursue dramatic writing at New York University (NYU) and to live in the city he had come to love, but this dream was shattered. Just before he left us, he tore up the portrait of New York City he had hung on the wall.

As a pacifist, David refused to compromise his convictions, and this was in keeping with his character. David has always been steadfast in his beliefs about right and wrong; it never sat well with him to bend to outside pressures—even when the rest of society and the government itself insisted he must bend. There is no doubt in my mind that my son's depression, which led to his death, stemmed from being forced to do something he found ethically repugnant, and about which his opinions and protests went unheard.

> *As a pacifist, David refused to compromise his convictions, and this was in keeping with his character.*

David was the victim of a bully. But that bully wasn't some schoolyard harasser who could be dealt with through parent-teacher meetings: it was the state. When bullying is state-sponsored, there is little one can do. It is legitimized through laws and common practices; it is "acceptable."

As the Human Rights Watch explains, "Singapore promotes itself as a bustling, modern city-state and a great place to do business. Beneath the slick surface of gleaming high-rises, however, it is a repressive place, where the government severely restricts what can be said, published, performed, read, or watched. Those who criticize the government or the judiciary, or publicly discuss race and religion, frequently find themselves facing criminal investigations and charges, or civil defamation suits and crippling damages."[8]

Attorney and scholar Jothie Rajah explores this phenomenon in her book, *Authoritarian Rule of Law: Legislation, Discourse, and*

---

8   "'Kill the Chicken to Scare the Monkeys': Suppression of Free Expression and Assembly in Singapore," Human Rights Watch, December 12, 2017, https://www.hrw.org/report/2017/12/12/kill-chicken-scare-monkeys/suppression-free-expression-and-assembly-singapore#.

Legitimacy in Singapore. In her book, she describes the ways in which authoritarian legalism has the capacity to create a seemingly liberal environment that actually "[constrains] dissent while augmenting discretionary political power."[9] In addition to her research, as the ex-wife of Singapore's minister for law and home affairs, K. Shanmugam, she has firsthand knowledge of government control.[10]

The bullying plays out in numerous ways—but primarily when it comes to free speech. Writers, bloggers, and activists have had their belongings seized and searched and even received prison time for speaking out. Public assemblies are also severely limited by law, targeting groups of any size—and even individuals—who attempt to express their opinion. For example, after the death of former prime minister Lee Kuan Yew, teen Amos Yee posted a video comparing Lee Kuan Yew to Jesus and describing them as "power-hungry and malicious." He spent a total of four weeks in prison for "wounding religious feelings" and obscenity charges.[11] Seelan Paley, a performance artist, spent two weeks in prison for violating the Public Order Act after staging a peaceful, one-man protest.[12] In 2018, Singapore amended its Public Order Act to further limit public assemblies—requiring permit applications a minimum of twenty-eight days in advance of any gathering and that police be notified of the expected turnout. The punishment? Fines up to USD$12,397, and/or up to a

---

9   Jothie Rajah, *Authoritarian Rule of Law: Legislation, Discourse and Legitimacy in Singapore*, Cambridge Studies in Law and Society (Cambridge: Cambridge University Press, 2012), i–vii.

10 Augustine Low, "The Hard Man of Singapore Politics," *The Independent*, April 2, 2018, http://theindependent.sg/the-hard-man-of-singapore-politics/.

11 "'Kill the Chicken to Scare the Monkeys.'"

12 "Singapore: Free Expression Targeted," Human Rights Watch, January 17, 2019, https://www.hrw.org/news/2019/01/17/singapore-free-expression-targeted#.

year in prison.[13]

In addition, in Singapore, LGBTQ people face not only discrimination but criminalization. Positive representations of LGBTQ people are severely censored, and consensual sex between men is still a criminal act.[14]

Where the laws are unjust or discriminatory, a democratic system allows remedies and adjustments. It is when the system is not democratic and pluralistic that unjust laws become everlasting tools for oppression and control by a small group of people. In places of freedom, a practice such as routine conscription—which has proven dangerous to the physical and mental health of young people—may have a chance of being abolished. But not here. Not in Singapore.

In my son's case, the state did not recognize the most fundamental of religious beliefs: pacifism. David's final act of civil disobedience should embolden us to give due recognition to the diversity of human life and beliefs. It is not for the state to draw lines in our spiritual beliefs. This is clearly discrimination—more than that, it is clear, unadulterated bullying.

> David's final act of civil disobedience should embolden us to give due recognition to the diversity of human life and beliefs.

When a person begins to comprehend to just what degree the Singaporean government is capable of browbeating and tormenting its young citizens, it becomes clear that they are not faultless when someone like David becomes depressed. It is easy to fathom how young people—on the cusp of beginning their adult lives, in which they will be expected to make

---

13   "Singapore 2017/2018," Amnesty International, accessed August 27, 2019, https://www.amnesty.org/en/countries/asia-and-the-pacific/singapore/report-singapore/.

14   "Singapore: Free Expression Targeted."

their own decisions—can become depressed when their autonomy is stripped from them.

Every eighteen-year-old male is forcibly conscripted by law in Singapore. That is to say, the youth is required to defend the country, and if necessary, to die for it. If this were not a demoralizing enough prospect in its own right, let us account for the fact that a conscripted youth is offered no voice whatsoever in the matter.

While the young men of Singapore are deemed adults for the purpose of military service at age eighteen, the government does not let them vote until they are twenty-one. It is presumed, in other words, that they are fit to die for their country before they are fit to speak up about it. To me it is natural that depression can result from this.

The American War of Independence in the eighteenth century erupted because of a similar act of bullying by the British monarch. The American colonies coined the phrase "no taxation without representation" and refused to pay taxes to the monarch if they did not have the right to a say in the government. The issue was an important enough one that they were willing to go war—understanding the likelihood that many lives would be lost in the process.

I consider this lack of representation one of the clear and present risk factors for depression in our young people and therefore something that should be changed immediately. Giving youth the right to vote *at least* by the age they could be conscripted is a step in the direction of ending this systemized bullying that traumatizes them.

While looking at these government issues is of critical importance, there are other factors as well that can be improved to prevent a death such as David's. In a father's efforts to understand and fulfill my son's wishes, I have learned a great deal about the practice of psychiatry in Singapore. What I've learned is that it, too, is in desperate need of a major overhaul.

* * *

> *Psychiatry is the branch of medicine focused on the diagnosis, treatment, and prevention of mental, emotional, and behavioral disorders. A psychiatrist is a medical doctor (an MD or DO) who specializes in mental health, including substance use disorders. Psychiatrists are qualified to assess both the mental and physical aspects of psychological problems.*
>
> **—American Psychiatric Association**

I contacted the APA after David left us. I learned a good deal from them about the professional and ethical codes to which their members are committed. I urge anyone seeking to learn more to contact them. The practice of psychiatry is a noble medical profession. But when it is abused—and in some instances, weaponized—every concern should be raised and addressed to ensure the crucial and productive role it performs in society is duly sustained.

To many patients, psychiatry is a potential lifesaver. Practitioners, patients, and the public at large must never lose sight of this. I am writing this as a father who had seen firsthand the failure not of psychiatry, the branch of medicine, but of the profession, where it related to my son. David experienced a business rather than a practice. He was treated by a businessman and not a practitioner of medical science.

After David's passing, I wrote to his psychiatrist, addressing the multitude of issues with David's treatment—including signs that there was a serious problem that went virtually unaddressed. I share a portion of that letter here so that readers can understand the kind of misconduct that can lead to tragedies like my family's. I also encourage anyone receiving counseling from a psychiatrist or psychologist to request to see their files. It will help shed light on whether the professional is doing their job.

While as David's father, I accept the responsibility for his passing, it rested in no small way on the fact I brought him to see you. That is a lesson I have since learned, painfully as it is—that psychiatry is not an exact science, and that some psychiatrists are nothing more than business people.

Since David's passing, I researched the practice of psychiatry. Going into the protocols of the American Psychiatric Association was sufficient for me to appreciate how little these protocols were adhered to by the psychiatric community.

I am also very disappointed in the way you attended—or didn't, rather—to David. David's view on this was also communicated to dear friends whom I heard from after his passing. Going through his file in your office after, I was especially surprised by two things:

1. Only a few sheets of written paper in the file, after ten months of consultations. An absence of a strategy or roadmap for treatment and cure was especially glaring.

2. David's confession to you that he had taken an overdose of his prescription medication in September 2015. I did not see anything in the file which showed alarm and urgent action on your part in respect to this. Also, there are practices in psychiatry wherein the family members are invited to participate in the sessions as a way to help resolve long-standing issues. This was one time where, given the state which David was in, you could have reached out to me.

Your failure and the stony silence on your face when I asked you why you did not inform me of the "overdose," led me to eventually research on the practice of psychiatry.

Add these to the final days when I tried to reach you urgently at your office upon learning David had taken another unacceptably large dosage. You called back several hours later and did not seem too concerned about this.

I take no pleasure in writing to you. I would prefer to forget that I had brought David to see you. However, I am constantly reminded of a poem which David wrote and which I found among his papers after he left us. The title was addressed to you. I assure you it was not a tribute.

You are kindly urged to practice your craft in a way which truly saves lives. I could not understand how a practice could have so many patients each day, clogging the office, and yet be able to really understand and attend to each unique individual patient. I am advised by a prominent psychiatrist that it's not possible. He further stated that three or four patients a day is ideal.

Thank you.

Yours sincerely,

Harmohan Singh

David's father

There was even less to commend about the approach of the Singaporean armed forces' psychiatrists, who assessed David separately. Their only purpose was to browbeat him into accepting conscription.

In general, by the time someone visits a psychiatrist, their underlying personal problems have become quite advanced. The patient desperately needs help. Because psychiatry is governed by a code of confidentiality, and because of the wide academic and professional literature available to the general population (especially through the internet), most prospective patients have very positive expectations of the treatment they will be receiving.

Contrary to the general perception, however, the practice of psychiatry anywhere in the world is problematic. This is functionally due to the fact that our brains, emotions, and behavior are extremely complex. As every thumbprint or strand of DNA is unique, so are our brains, emotions, and spirits. So are *we*.

The code of ethics to which every psychiatrist is duty-bound supports the idea that every individual is unique, valid, and worthwhile. Every patient is a life to be saved! More than nearly any other type of profession, this one embodies a sacred duty. Every doctor is aware of this—though, regrettably, some take it less seriously than others.

I will reiterate: psychiatry is a noble medical profession. It has helped millions across the globe. Because of its intrusively personal nature, however, psychiatry may be abused to suit purposes that have nothing to do with the welfare of the patient, such as:

- Monetary gain for the practitioner at the expense of adequate care for the patient

- A political tool to be used by the state against its opponents

- Weaponization for war or torture

- Control of a general population or individual by the state or colonial entity

Whenever psychiatry is used for any of the purposes named

above, a serious breach of ethics occurs.

Like any medical field, psychiatry is always evolving. But while this is occurring, societal and social problems also evolve. New problems lead to new insights and treatment. And so it goes.

Psychiatry continues to offer comfort and stability to many. It is because of this promise that the practice of psychiatry must strive to retain its foundational essence—the professional treatment and care of an individual who needs help, without qualification as to means, gender, race, or nationality.

As I mentioned in the first chapter, David wrote a play about his last interview with the Singaporean armed forces' psychiatrists. It was not a tribute. Titled *Property of this Country*, it was heartbreaking for me to read after my son had left us. I have taken it upon myself to ensure that this play—along with David's other works—is published in due time so that others are made aware of what truly goes on in these instances.

For David, being a conscientious objector came from deep inside. It defined him. You can't redefine someone like David by force, nor should this be attempted—but it is apparent to me that the armed forces' psychiatrists tried to. Rather than considering and responding to his actual mental state, they tried to overturn his core beliefs with propaganda and force. They toyed with the life of a promising, kind, loving, and vulnerable youth—and in so doing abandoned their code of ethics altogether. They abandoned their humanity.

The term psychiatry was first coined by the German physician Johann Christian Reil in 1808, and literally means the medical treatment of the soul.

—Wikipedia (accessed May 23, 2018)

Perhaps this is why psychiatry is not an exact science. We must always keep this in mind about psychiatrists, including those who "assessed" David. Brainwashing has no more legitimate a place in psychiatry than business—both are abuses of an essential human service.

Psychiatry is an intrusive exercise into the life of a willing subject. An exercise designed to help and to restore the mental and physiological well-being of the subject. *Trust* in the doctor is a critical factor in the treatment, and this trust must always be respected and honored by the psychiatrist.

Since the dawn of modern psychiatry more than two hundred years ago, its practice has gone through significant changes as medical science has advanced. Unlike other medical disciplines, however, psychiatry has a dual dimension—that is, it can be used in two different ways, for two different purposes. The first is a medical practice, to restore the health of the patient. The second is a contrived abuse of trust, to control and dominate the subject for personal or political reasons.

It is the second dimension that concerns me, because I believe this is what was done to David.

Any patient who is receiving less than adequate professional attention and treatment is being abused. Such a patient is akin to a customer who pays hundreds of dollars for a new iPhone without realizing they had been sold a knockoff. Should any customer accept this knowingly? There are laws against this practice, which is properly called *fraud*.

In psychiatry, it can be difficult to determine whether the patient is not receiving adequate professional care—in most cases. Sometimes, however, the abuse is so gross that it becomes obvious to outside parties. In most cases, the doctor is accountable primarily to himself or herself for being conscientious in practice. It is critical, for the sake of the patient, who places their faith and their very life in the hands of a stranger, that the doctor take this responsibility seriously.

In February 2018, the NGO Human Rights Watch (HRW) published an investigation of nursing homes in the United States titled "Nursing Homes Misuse Drugs to Control Residents." This publication is readily available online, and I urge everyone to review it.[15]

The questions raised by this shocking publication: Who are these medical practitioners who routinely prescribe antipsychotic drugs to the residents? Who are the ones torturing these helpless senior citizens for monetary gain? And perhaps most important, what is being done to put an end to this? In other words, where is the accountability?

These are pertinent questions to which I have no ready answers, particularly as I am a layman. My initial thought is to apply something like the RICO law that is applied to organized crime in the United States. The Racketeer Influenced and Corrupt Organizations Act (RICO) is a federal law enacted in 1970 to facilitate the prosecution of organized criminal networks like the Mafia.

In Singapore, we have no equivalent protection: laws against corporate crimes are weak and not systematically enforced. Any damages and awards for victims are negligible compared to those dispensed in similar cases in the United States. Elsewhere in this book, I have depicted Singapore as a multinational corporate state; the land belongs to corporations—as does the law. Our law regarding class-action lawsuits is weak to nonexistent, because it is more concerned with the rights and privileges of state and private oligarchic corporations than with those of individuals.

---

15 "Nursing Homes Misuse Drugs to Control Residents," Human Rights Watch, February 5, 2018, https://www.hrw.org/news/2018/02/05/us-nursing-homes-misuse-drugs-control-residents.

As with most problems in Singapore, this one is layered. For something like the RICO law to be leveraged against corrupt psychiatrists, we would first have to accept the idea that the law, at its essence, is intended to protect the rights of individuals—not corporations and those acting as mouthpieces for the government.

For *that* to happen, people would need to be aware of the pervasiveness of government-backed abuse. This is nearly impossible when the press is gagged. People remain unaware of how corporations trample on individuals and of the severity of the problems in the medical community. This ignorance works in favor of public officials and their sponsors. A free press is that critical first step toward solving this and many other problems in Singapore.

As it stands now, people have been told for generations that our health care system is among the best in the world. If I cannot effectively dispute that assessment, it's because we have no independent means of measuring and comparing our success—all pertinent raw data is withheld by the state.

The problems with the medical care system itself (SingHealth) are numerous. First, it is thoroughly enmeshed in the government—meaning its management is answerable to the same corporate interests and prone to the same issues that characterize our government as a whole. SingHealth's CEO, Ivy Ng, is married to the country's minister of defense, Ng Eng Hen. In addition, the prime minister—Lee Hsien Loong—is married to Ho Ching, the CEO and executive director of Temasek Holdings, Singapore's sovereign wealth fund. As long-serving executives, each party draws millions in salary annually. For leading Singapore, which is really no bigger than a city, Prime Minister Loong is paid $1.7 million per year.[16] The unelected

---

16   Amarendra Bhushan Dhiraj, "These are the 20 Highest Paid Political Leaders in the World in 2018," *CEOWorld Magazine*, April 24, 2018, https://ceoworld.biz/2018/

president of Singapore, Halimah Yacob, is compensated handsomely as well, at $1.54 million.[17]

Our health care system is also a tourist draw! While SingHealth's hospitals and clinics are for citizens and permanent residents, there are thousands of well-heeled Indonesians, Malaysians, Vietnamese, Filipinos, and Papuans who flock to Singapore's private hospitals and clinics, since every medical institution must comply with the requirements and guidelines of the ministry of health. Lured to Singapore by the comparatively low costs of many major procedures, practitioners determined to appeal to an international clientele, and our urban development relative to much of Asia, these *medical tourists* represent a substantial consumer demographic—which the government bends to accommodate as much as possible.

You can see the ways in which medical systems like Singapore's may be abused for political ends, and psychiatry and psychology are not exempt. This was exemplified by the abuses routinely carried out in the old Soviet Union. Dissidents and political opponents of the regime were incarcerated in mental institutions—the objective being to discredit them. This is *bullying* in its rawest form. Nothing is more disturbing than people in power abusing their privilege by harming helpless citizens.

To be clear, there have been many cases of abuse of this nature.

04/24/these-are-the-20-highest-paid-political-leaders-in-the-world-in-2018/.

17 "Remuneration for Ministers and Members of Parliament," Public Service Division, Prime Minister's Office, Singapore Government, accessed October 16, 2019, http://www.ifaq.gov.sg/psd/apps/fcd_faqmain.aspx?qst=hRhkP9BzcBKn t75r%2Bl1bopmAANxUYJsZ1XtCavhh%2Bg8uifs%2FSSJBsHDTcHJB1%2FKdJEcau dLZZH80Azo7UxJvw21ao65qKq3tvdU1YT5vbbQ%2Bvz2gBNUuTEU9RYYbiXjcxxx 1iuuCkEH58vl2LdFXxxSW45Ci62%2Fi#FAQ_34324. Remarkably, this is a drastic reduction, in the face of public scrutiny, of the previous salary of over $4.2 million (Faris Mokhtar, "Singapore President's annual salary tops S$4.2 million," Yahoo News, March 11, 2011, https://sg.news.yahoo.com/singapore-president-s-annual-salary-tops-s-4-2-million-.html.

The United States has also suffered its share of abuses for political purposes. For example, back in 1953, the CIA launched a program titled Project MKUltra. What began as an attempt to keep pace with the Soviet Union's efforts to utilize mind control became a broader effort to "[use] biological and chemical materials [to alter] human behavior."[18] The project included illegal drug testing on unknowing and often vulnerable subjects, such as prisoners and those with terminal cancers. When the truth about the program came to light, the American people were shocked and incredulous. But it wasn't the end of covert and abusive practices like these.

Since the tragedy of 9/11 in 2001, the US government is alleged to have collaborated with psychologists on the design of torture techniques and procedures for its Global War on Terrorism.

The abuse of psychiatry, especially its weaponization against political opponents and in war, is a grave injustice. This must be brought to an end immediately, and those medical professionals involved in it must be held accountable for their crimes.

The practice of psychiatry is at a tipping point. The medical community can either deal resolutely with the abuses perpetrated by its members, or it can continue to plod along, deluding itself that the problem is not pervasive.

A reminder: a single life *is* sacred. Thousands of lives are put at risk daily. Are we attending to the practice of psychiatry with a view to the sanctity of the profession?

No doubt there are good doctors in the community who are addressing the problem. But the fact that psychiatry is one of the fastest-growing professions in our society today attests that there are too many damaged

---

18   Kat Eschner, "What We Know About the CIA's Midcentury Mind-Control Project," Smithsonian.com, April 13, 2017, https://www.smithsonianmag.com/smart-news/what-we-know-about-cias-midcentury-mind-control-project-180962836/.

individuals in society. Just look at the opioid crisis in the West. There's one too in Singapore, except we don't have freedom of the press, and therefore we are not generally aware of the problem unless we live in the Geylang-Jalan Sultan areas—or unless we visit the office of a psychiatrist and observe the large number of teenaged patients there!

With the vast problems—and unhealthy ways to escape them—laid at the feet of our young people in modern times, we have to be more vigilant than ever. We have to look at what treatment options genuinely exist for them. We have to take them seriously when they show signs of depression; in this restrictive society, it can affect anyone. As we look at ourselves and the world around us, we must ask a haunting but critical question:

What are we doing to our kids?

* * *

David always lived by what he believed. His beliefs, moreover, were simple and straightforward—a sensible way for beliefs to be. This is much more than I can say for myself. David was and is my teacher.

By his final act, David hoped I would be spurred to action. By this final act, his destiny and mine intertwined forever, just like a binary star. He knew this. He commanded that I should continue his work. And part of that work is to shed light—for all those who will see it—on the need for change in the Singaporean system. That system needs to be able to deal with the very real depression its young people do face, and will continue facing, in response to conscription, which robs these young people of their individuality while enforcing that their only worth can be found in the context of service to the country. Depression will naturally develop when young people believe that their moral objections and their highest values simply do not matter.

CHAPTER 7

Answers and Activism for David

Of David's countless positive attributes, the primary one I think of when I reflect on his life is his pacifism. To me, pacifism is the deepest and purest expression of our humanity, and this was David through and through. Never one to pay lip service to some ideal while living his own life apart from his standards, David made his decisions according to his own high standards. At the same time, his beliefs were simple and straightforward—as any code of moral conduct should be. His final request of me, the instruction that would give shape to my own journey, was that I continue his work—his legacy. In the time since his passing, I have made it my primary occupation to honor that code of conduct.

> *Never one to pay lip service to some ideal while living his own life apart from his standards, David made his decisions according to his own high standards. At the same time, his beliefs were simple and straightforward—as any code of moral conduct should be.*

In June 2017, I visited the United States for two weeks to begin the process of creating the book you are reading. I came away from this productive visit with two vital realizations:

1. The book about my beloved son was becoming a reality.
2. The causes he cared about—freedom, human rights, pacifism, LGBTQ rights, the rights of conscientious objectors, the rights of people with mental health issues, etc.—needed additional attention.

My previous travels and even my own college years had already familiarized me, to an extent, with the culture of the United States—I already understood well how Singaporean culture disappointed by contrast. My June 2017 visit revived the comparison and lent it a new level of lucidity.

The very rights my son had fought for in Singapore—basic rights, but peerless in their importance to human dignity—were openly discussed and celebrated in the United States. Seeing the cultural embodiment of my son's highest values in living color made it clearer than ever: I needed to continue David's activism.

This facet of my journey would take the form of blogging about human rights issues, which I continue to do frequently via the blog which David's family and friends created in his memory. It is appropriately named *Think to See,* in the truest essence of David and what he stood for. The blog may be accessible as follows: www.thinktosee.tumblr.com.

Throughout his campaign for human rights, autonomy, and dignity—an effort that permeated every area of his life—David always posited that peace is not possible for people who live in fear. My journey to the United States highlighted just how right he was. David knew he would find peace in the United States; the country was his beacon, as it was and is for millions in the world.

When Americans reflect on their own politics and great culture, they frequently focus on faults. Citizens of the United States may cite their philosophical factions, their disagreement on hot-topic political issues, and their disharmony on any number of other matters. But coming from a country that devalues individual freedom, I have observed in the United States a form of harmony that transcends perfect concurrence on *the issues*.

> *Throughout his campaign for human rights, autonomy, and dignity—an effort that permeated every area of his life—David always posited that peace is not possible for people who live in fear.*

The United States, like my son, has struggled for freedom. Americans—from San Francisco to Washington, DC, Nashville, and New York City—guard their hard-won freedom passionately. Every individual I met during my stay impressed me with their sense of civic duty and appreciation for the values of freedom and free speech enshrined in their Constitution.

Every American, I realized, is a *human rights activist!*

There are other countries that are similarly dedicated to upholding the rights of their citizens, of course. Norway, in particular, comes to mind. In September of 2016, King Harald V of Norway delivered a speech supporting the rights of LGBT people and refugees and stressing the importance of tolerance. I wrote to him expressing my gratitude for his words, as well as their potential impact on so many people. I wrote:

> Your Majesty,
>
> Your speech is most welcome and refreshing.
>
> It shows courage and great leadership.
>
> Our son, David, who passed away in Feb. this year, would have been pleased. He believed strongly in freedom and the right of every individual to a life of peace and the pursuit of her dreams. He stood by his ideals right to the end.
>
> It is hoped, with your loving speech and support, many more individuals like David in the world could live their dreams.

About a month later, I received a letter from Tormod C. Endresen, the ambassador of Norway to Singapore. He disclosed that he had passed my letter on to the king and shared his opinion on the matter, writing, "On my own account, I would like to thank you for sharing the story of your son David's life. I fully agree that we must strive for a world where tolerance reigns and where all individuals are allowed to be who they are. This is also why Norway in January this year, during the Universal Periodic Review in the UN Human Rights Council encouraged Singapore to abolish the provision that makes homosexuality illegal in Singapore."

We in Singapore must aspire to do better for ourselves and our children, to fight for human rights, like Americans and so many others do. We have to take back what is rightfully ours and give unto Caesar that which is his. This was my son's ideal, and he did his part to make it a reality. He did not isolate any realm of his life from his activism.

If society as a whole is to follow my son's brave example—championing, as he did, a better world for every Singaporean—we need to fight the widespread system of brainwashing that defines the culture today. In chapter 8, I look in detail at the institutions—from the military to public schooling to psychiatry—which further this agenda. It is my wish to summarize here some of the efforts I've taken since David's passing to learn of the specific ways in which these institutions failed my son, as they are failing others, and to hold them responsible.

Because I consider it important to keep a record, accessible to myself and others, of my attempts to communicate with those in a position to change things (and because I understand that my chances of receiving any response to direct communication are slim to nonexistent), I have begun writing open letters, which I have posted on the *Think to See* blog. By now there are far too many to include in this book, but I will present here one of great importance:

October 27, 2017

Dr. Ng Eng Hen, Defense Minister, Singapore

Dear Sir,

RE: David Cornelius Singh—A Life; Protection for the Vulnerable Youth

This has reference to my several letters to you, including those dated Apr 14, May 29 and July 14, 2017:

A. The Background

I raised with you a few important issues that remain unaddressed by the armed forces. These include:

1. Legal protection for Conscientious Objectors (CO). My son, David took his life because he was a CO. Since his passing, I have proposed that legislation be enacted to recognize CO. For your guidance, one of the most admired people in history was the legendary Muhammed Ali. He was a CO. He suffered for his beliefs and yet stood his ground. So did David.

Regrettably, there has not been any reply from you on this life-saving aspect.

2. Legal protection, including disruption (exemption) from service for conscripts with mental health issues. This includes those who are yet to be conscripted but have been medically ascertained to be struggling with mental health problems. David suffered from depression because of his impending conscription.

Also, no substantive reply from you on this proposal.

3. Objective and impartial medical assessment for every pre-enlistee/conscript. I have pointed out to you in my letters that the current protocols employed by the armed forces are neither objective nor independent and are certainly inadequate toward the interest of our youth who are being assessed. This cannot be denied.

Still, no substantive reply from you.

I have also proposed that the armed forces should not directly employ or retain medical personnel who are assessing pre-enlistees. This is to preclude conflicts of interest and to assure the integrity of the assessment, and further promote/sustain the welfare of the patients/assessed. To date, this has not been addressed, to my knowledge.

4. National Service/Conscription—I have stated (and you have not denied) that it is less about the "defense" of Singapore and more about the political socialization of our youth. I have proposed that we regularize our armed forces into a professional service, as Taiwan did.

I have also said (and you have not denied) that Singapore is a NATO-East base of operations. Therefore, it is unlikely the island faces any military threat from its neighbors due to the presence of nuclear and advanced NATO-East weapons and other so-called foreign military assets on and around Singapore.

However, as I also mentioned, the presence of NATO-East military forces opens Singapore to a ballistic missile strike from outside the region in event of regional or global hostilities. This is Singapore's true vulnerability, which no conscript can be reasonably expected to counter. This was the same scenario in WW2 when Imperial Japan attacked and occupied Singapore because the British Empire's Far East operations were centered on the island.

B. A Citizen and Former Conscript's (service Apr 1978 to Oct 1980) Request for Information

I refer you to reports of suicides in the Israeli armed forces, especially among the conscripts.

I am requesting the following information; in considering this, please bear in mind a state is not above the people but instead serves them.

1. Number of suicides in the Singapore armed forces in the last 10 years, expressed in annual terms.

2. Number of attempted suicides for the same period and model.

3. Number of conscripts and/or pre-enlistees who were disrupted/discharged/waived from military service for medical reasons during the same period and model.

4. Number of conscripts and pre-enlistees who suffered from mental health issues who were waived or disrupted/downgraded for the same period and model.

I look forward to your soonest and favorable reply to the proposals and requests contained in this letter.

C. Conclusion

Conscientious objection is the very foundation of religious and spiritual authority! It is an uncompromising belief in nonviolence. Gandhi brought a bully, the British Empire, to its knees with this. It's about time we educated our children and youth about nonviolence and peaceful, rather than violent and militarized actions, which only serve to foster the interest of those who rule.

This is the 50th year of military conscription and militarized education for our youth. Contrary to the official line, there is nothing to celebrate over this two-year program, which is apparently aimed at controlling the minds and behavior of our youth.

As I stated before, our youth have dreams. It is not for you to take these dreams—and with that, their identities—away for your purpose.

By Ministry of External Affairs (GODL-India), GODL-India, https://commons.wikimedia.org/w/index.php?curid=71847638

This letter was posted in October 2017. As of the writing of this book, there has been no response. None to the numerous, critical issues I outlined in section A and none to the request by a grieving father for relevant data, as outlined in section B.

In a letter dated April 14, 2017 (Good Friday), to the Singaporean defense minister, I had already brought up my belief that military conscription has never been about defense, as well as one of the points you can read in section C of the preceding letter—that the true purpose of national service is the uniformity and conformity of our youth.

To: Minister, Defense. Singapore—Dr. Ng Eng Hen

12 Pages

April 14, 2017

Dear Sir,

RE: David Cornelius Singh—A Life

I have received the email dated Mar. 16, 2017 from the permanent secretary.

To say I am disappointed is a gross understatement. David's family has been most patient over the year this has taken. A simple request for a meeting, a PROMISE given, and yet never honoured by the SAF.

We have reached its end through no fault of ours, and despite all the difficult and clearly unsuccessful efforts of the family aimed at engaging you and the organization which you lead. I could not reconcile, try as I did, your inaction and insensitivity, to the speech given by the PM in parliament previously about political leadership of "high quality, accountable (responsive), honest, competent and effective."

What happened? Let's find out:

A. Let Me First Address the Perm Sec's Letter:

1. It is not true to state that the Singapore Armed Forces is "unable to accede to your request." The fact is this:

You had acceded to our request early last year. You have since been avoiding our several efforts to materialize this promise you made. The prolonged delays are nothing short of a cynical and shameful attempt to forestall the family in the hope that the matter will blow away over time.

2. The family has been seeking a meeting, and also to receive David's true medical report. You have not complied as promised

and have not taken the matter seriously. I say this because we had written to you personally after exhausting every possible endeavour on email over several months with the Commander, CMPB regarding our request. He had demonstrated his word meant little. Yet, you did not personally see fit to reply to our letter and instead, a nameless bureaucrat was tasked to respond to us.

This is about a LIFE. My son's life. And I am left to communicate with someone who would not reveal his name, nor actively engage us and went under the benign-sounding title of "permanent secretary." Don't you think all these colonial protocols should have been thrown out in 1965 when we came into our own? How much more insensitive and uncaring can the state be?

3. As a consequence of your inaction and complete silence, the family sent a letter to the PM, again requesting the SAF to honour its promise to the family. I am therefore startled that the PM did not reply too, and the family received a response instead by email from the same nameless bureaucrat stating the matter was being looked into. Suffice, after this, there was nothing further from the bureaucrat. The family had to once more send reminders to him for a reply. He then gave a final and unhelpful response which I referenced earlier.

4. Please compare your deliberate inaction and silence to the speedy response initiated by the SAF when a few of its armoured troop carriers were legally seized recently in HK. All manner of SAF, state and state-sponsored public relations resources were immediately deployed to engage the HK local government to

resolve this matter favourably and at the same time to keep our public apprised generally.

The take-away from this troop carrier matter, from David's family's standpoint, is a Life of a Citizen, a child at that, means nothing when compared to a few war machines. This is the state of our SAF. The root problem as always, is not the good people who serve tirelessly in it, but its leadership or more precisely, lack of.

This leadership gives practical meaning to the term, "Take Cover!"

B. I Shall Now Address the Matter of Who David Was:

1. David suffered from clinical depression. Your medical officers knew of this. It started from the year before his passing, due to the anxiety he felt about his impending conscription to the SAF.

2. During David's first check-up at the Manpower Base (CMPB), I received a telephone call from your medical officer informing me, David had self-harmed that morning. The medical officer would not release him to go home alone. He requested my presence immediately to take my son home. I went there right away and fetched David. This is a vital warning sign which was subsequently ignored by the SAF. To say the least, his situation was precarious and caution should have been applied foremost in everything concerning him and especially how he might react or not, to "triggers."

3. David was a Conscientious Objector. I am told by a person who said he no longer worked for the state that, "there's no such thing as a conscientious objector" in Singapore. I beg to differ. David proved there is. With his life! I am not concerned with the

"rule of law," especially where it relates to whose rule and whose law. This is a question of David's Life and his Human Rights which were shamelessly denied him, and which you should be reminded, are sacred! This is above all a moral and sacred matter.

4. During David's last medical assessment, it is my understanding from him that he informed the doctor in very clear terms that he was a conscientious objector. He also stated that he would take his Life if the SAF drafted him. He made it abundantly clear it did not matter under what vocation he would be serving, it would still be going against his conscience. Also, I was initially invited to attend this review with David. The SAF subsequently informed me my presence was not necessary.

Why was this?

Who made this decision?

5. David came home from this assessment visibly upset. He told me the doctor was abrasive and was incapable of appreciating his concerns and his diversity. A transcript of this encounter was made by David. I found this only after his passing while going through his papers. He titled it, "Property of This Country." We can imagine what he went through with these insensitive and irresponsible medical practitioners. They were more interested in "breaking" him—to get him to accept military conscription, rather than to perform a final and completely objective assessment of his mental and emotional state. No wonder the family was denied the meeting with these doctors. Is this the reason why the SAF also rejected our request for his real medical report?

It breaks my heart to read what my son had to go through with these misguided doctors, who were clearly more into mind-control than medical care. A young patient's trust was no doubt grossly and tragically abused.

6. David was a gentle and caring boy. He was the brightest and most courageous person. He dared to speak his mind where others, especially I, lived in fear of the State. David had Dreams. He wanted to study in Cambridge or New York University. According to his teachers, he would have no problems getting in. He was very talented. He scored 44 out of a possible 45 points for the IB exams, and he received the "Theatre Prize" from his high school.

At 16 years, David won 2nd prize in a national script-writing competition. His script, "Piety" was published in a compendium by the organizer. David collected royalties. He was so happy. At this tender age, he had already accomplished much more than I, his father, ever had all my life. He would have done Singapore and, Humanity proud anywhere. He was on his way to great and good things, primarily because he was Very Sure of himself. He told me, "Be yourself!" David worked so hard for all these.

7. David was gay. He cared deeply about the rights of LGBTQ people everywhere. He attended the annual Pink Dot event since 2013. He felt discrimination in any form, especially through the law, was nothing short of Bullying. This included Singapore's Penal Code Section 377A criminalizing all gay persons (and in the process, denying them their civil rights. Never mind that the state says it does not enforce the law. So much more reason to scrap it). This law is yet again, another colonial hold-over. David felt strongly that overcoming discrimination requires an unwavering commitment to free speech. He would never compromise

on this as we tragically and painfully found out. His passing was a final act of civil disobedience.

C. I Will Now Address the Question of the Inaction of SAF and Your Deliberate Failure to Honour Your Promise to the Family.

1. Judging from the way the SAF (and the state) handled David's matter before and after his passing, it is very clear there is a total absence of leadership, ownership, and accountability. This is negligence in the worst possible way, especially given an organization tasked with national defense and the care of our conscripts. It has been a year, and yet, the family continues to be stonewalled.

Where is the moral responsibility and ownership of the matter within the SAF and the state?

Where is the active engagement with the family?

The matter of David's passing was left to a nameless bureaucrat to communicate on email with the family, and poorly at that.

2. Five days after David's passing, and three days after he was to be conscripted, we received a telephone call from someone in CMPB. He asked where David was. When informed by David's sister, Sara that he had passed away, the person asked for proof! He wanted a copy of the death certificate. Sara sent this over immediately. Nothing further was heard from CMPB or the SAF until we contacted them a few weeks later to commence our request for a meeting with the people who interviewed him last. No expression of condolences from CMPB before then. This callous regard for David and his memory, from the SAF would continue throughout the period of our many (and I should add,

emotionally painful and difficult) attempts to engage the organization in respect of our request for the meeting and to gain access to the medical report.

3. The SAF medical professionals who interviewed David last have failed to step forward to identify themselves, and to meet with the family as requested. They have shown scant regard for Life.

Whatever happened to the Hippocratic oath?

Is this dispensed with in the SAF?

Where is the compassion? And these are doctors?

Moreover, their report is denied to the family.

Again, what sort of leadership is this? What example are we setting for our youthful conscripts and their concerned families? Are the lives of our youth in the hands of desk-bound generals who are more adept at politicking and stonewalling, than leading? Nothing could be more irresponsible than this.

4. Please do not take exception to what I just said. You have as much acknowledged this yourself through the employment of not SAF personnel, but foreign mercenaries to protect your homes and workplaces (again another colonial hold-over). Obviously, the SAF personnel are not good enough to protect you and your family? What kind of example have you been setting? I just cannot understand this picture—a defense minister being protected by foreign mercenaries.

Do you not have confidence and trust in the organization and the citizen-soldiers which you lead? And you accused and persecuted your critics for allegedly insulting the sensibilities of the People? What is this then?

Please do not tell me these mercenaries from Nepal are exclusive warriors. This racialist thinking originated from the colonials. Please bear in mind that during WW2, when the Imperial Japanese forces advanced into Singapore, these warrior-mercenaries, along with all the allied colonial forces surrendered although they far out-numbered (and out-gunned) the Japanese. But wait, someone did not surrender—the Malay Regiment, consisting of just 42 professional and indigenous soldiers, fought courageously for 2 days to the last man. And please learn about how their leader, Lt. Adnan died horribly at the hands of the Japanese. This was truly a leader. He led from the front. Not from the back and certainly not from behind a desk.

And now, We, the People are told no local civil society and dissident are permitted to be sponsored and supported by foreigners or a foreign organization? Is it another matter when it concerns you? Where is the equality of the law? I am sorry for being blunt, but please appreciate these are just plain facts. I am trying to get to the bottom of how far this irresponsible leadership extends to, because my son's Life is gone and there is a good possibility the precious lives of more Singaporean youth may already be put at risk because of this.

5. I have been a dutiful citizen for all my life. But I now realize there is a distinction between being dutiful for the sake of the country and being obedient to a self-serving and long-embedded ruling class. It took David's passing for me to realize this difference. A very painful lesson, for a father. I do not wish this for anyone. Not at all.

6. I shall be addressing in the future the question of protecting conscientious objectors and pre-enlistees with mental health issues, by way of law. The current position is proved to be grossly deficient and does not serve the overall public interest. Also, I would like to raise the issue of the standard needed for the vulnerable youth to be exempted from National Service. I do not accept the "severity concept." There have been too many suicides. Transparent policies must be in place that wherever a youth attends an interview at the Manpower Base, his basic human rights to be safe are fully acknowledged and secured. This is a question of life. I would encourage you and the state to support this initiative by the family for the common good of Singapore so we may be a beacon for compassion and care for our vulnerable youth. I shall call this David's Law.

7. Additionally, every medical consultant to the SAF should NOT be employed, retained and paid directly by the SAF or the state. This is to ensure the independence of their medical assessment and to allow them to do their critically life-protecting job objectively and without favour to the SAF or the state. I will be making specific proposals on operationalizing and orchestrating this. And, I have no interest in a committee of rubber-stampers and sycophants for this exercise if one is called for, because obviously, nothing substantive will come out of it. I had witnessed enough over the decades.

D. I Will Now Address Briefly the Question of the System of Governance in Singapore Which Had a Bearing on David's Passing

1. My daughter, Sara and I have lost a brother and a son. It is a very hard thing to accept, especially when David was so young

and had his future ahead of him. I should have taken him away from Singapore. I failed him, no doubt. This is a sacred trust a child places in his parent. His Life. It is something I have to live with the rest of my life.

2. During David's memorial, I spoke to family and friends in attendance—I said I feared the law of man more than I feared God's law. It is because of this that I lost my son. I should have taken David away! It would have been the godly thing to do—to save a life, my son's life.

3. My son gave his life so we may come to our senses and act to address the sad state of governance in Singapore, including the forced military conscription which appears to create uniformity and conformity among the youth rather than toward the purpose of the defense of the country. I had questioned the purpose of military conscription and its "political socialization" factor in a letter to you long before David's passing. I received a reply from a bureaucrat reading me the party line. Again, no active engagement with a concerned citizen. Nor does the system responsibly address the question of good citizens who are conscientious objectors and or suffer from mental health problems. These issues are present because the political system is self-serving. No one dares to speak their mind and We the People, have understandably lost our sense of initiative to question the government when the need arises, which I say to you, should be done every day. This is what checks and balance mean in a democracy, and not a rubber-stamped, yet overpaid parliament and state-owned, euthanized main stream press.

Related to the above, please explain how is it a youth is old enough to be conscripted at 18 years, and if necessary to die defending his country, but not old or mature enough to vote? This is clearly taxation without representation, for a start. Only a bully would do this.

4. David could have been saved if we had a free political system. The medical doctors assessing him then would likely be clear in their approach to medical practice, primarily because in an open and engaging system, We, the People would have been actively involved in the development of an independent sourcing system for medical practitioners toward assessing our youth's suitability for conscription.

5. It is time we overhauled our system of governance—50 years is long enough, with colonial laws and practices (British and Japanese) still present, held together by what appears to be a Club of self-serving leaders. A disgrace to our country's declared independence, by any measure.

And now, just look at the office of the Singapore President. 99.99 percent of the people are disqualified by your law to stand for this "elected" position. Do you fellas ever read the Universal Declaration of Human Rights (UDHR)? I guess not. And last I checked, Singapore is a member of the United Nations, to which the referenced document originated. Please read, learn and accede to all the human rights conventions, and cease to foment embarrassing excuses about "form" vs substance. Please, for the sake of our Country and People.

The UDHR was launched in 1948. A time when most parts of the world, including Singapore were under colonial rule. It was the inspiration for the millions of people at that time who were living under tyranny and colonial occupation. People who struggled with their lives to be free. Many lost their lives as a result.

Did our forebears not struggle against tyranny that you felt we had no need for this document?

Or did we replace a colonial power with a self-serving group?

Please enlighten me on this.

6. Back to NS—A fully professionalized defense force, based on real operational performance, and led by generals with substance, would be a more effective solution to our country's security. Just look at the Taiwan example. Taiwan is an island which faces a major security threat from the mainland. They obviously knew the best way to defend themselves was to scrap forced conscription and to professionalize. And please do not tell me what it would cost to mount this. If we can pay you so much more than any cabinet member anywhere in the world, why can't we adequately pay our professional soldiers for something so noble as our country's defence? (Please be reminded Singapore is no bigger than most major cities of the world, to the extent our leaders should in all fairness, be paid in accordance with that which the mayors of these cities receive). And do not tell me there would be a manpower crunch if we professionalized. What is the use of giving citizenship to millions of people from abroad if we cannot entice them to commit to something as noble as the defense of their new land?

To top all these, we have what I have termed "NATO East," centered in Singapore. United States, Canada, West Europe, Australia and NZ forces and assets are based and rotated here regularly. Who in his right mind would want to harm Singapore? Our nearest neighbours, Indonesia, Malaysia and Thailand are part of the Western alliance to which Singapore too belongs. The only real threat we face is a hypersonic nuclear missile strike from outside S.E. Asia to neutralize the assets and forces of our Western allies here in the event of global hostilities. And what can a conscript do about this? Stand there, with a rifle in hand, and be vaporized along with everyone else on the island, while a few, privileged families would have flown the coop by then?

7. I am left to conclude this self-serving behaviour is the cause of your decision not to honour your promise to David's family. This is the price we pay for our non-democratic political system and institutions. I am all too aware of your fear of Democracy. Is it because you lack confidence in yourself and your leadership?

David's was not the first, and going by the way this system operates, his will not be the last.

Conclusion

1. David's family is still waiting for you to honour your promise to give us access to those medical professionals who interviewed him last and also for his true medical report, and not the sanitized, 3rd party summary which you furnished. We hope to receive your favourable reply by May 05, 2017.

2. I reserve the right to share our communication (this letter, the others before and all emails) with all stakeholders as I am obliged to think necessary, just as I know you do with your various state bodies, secret police (still another colonial edifice), euthanized mass media and out-sourced PR and legal shops. This is about David's Life—his human rights. It is not the sole purview of the state. Every human being in this world is a stakeholder when it touches on the issue of human rights anywhere. It is about our humanity! We cannot draw boundaries on the question of our

humanity, for then we are saying we are less than human, or at least the ones doing the drawing.

And certainly, I do not wish for David's passing to be lost within a Weberian system as yours.

3. You may take exception to the contents of this letter. That is your right. It is perhaps time for you to experience a little free speech from a commoner, yet still a citizen nevertheless. Free Speech is sacred. Should you or the State decide to persecute me (now or later) and or David's family as a consequence, that is a right too, which you had long ago undemocratically arrogated to yourself exclusively. Allow me however, to paraphrase Sir Winston Churchill when he addressed the Nazis of Germany on the eve of WW2:

You do your worst, and we shall do our best.

4. As a result of David's passing, the SAF now reportedly allows NS men to choose their vocations. While this is positive, it does not go far enough to address the fundamental issues of the diversity and sanctity of human life and beliefs, including the human rights and safety of our "at risk" youth which I raised above. I shall be following up on this with a view to ensuring adequate and reasonable protection, within international standards, for our youth.

David said just before his passing that he'd choose the path he eventually took so others after him, may be free to pursue their dreams unhindered. I intend to progress this vigorously, in memory of David and what he stood for. He had more balls than the desk-bound generals and sycophants which our cynical rulers surround yourselves with. David lived by his ideals, right to the end. He had little patience for insecure, spoilt, arrogant and self-serving people who call themselves "realists." He knew there was nothing real about opportunists.

5. National Service is not just about putting on a uniform. It is about serving the country in any capacity. Every day, everywhere on the island, Singaporeans of every age and gender perform their national service to the country—we work, go to school, study, pay our taxes, volunteer, are law-abiding, look after our loved ones, have children, and more. This is National Service. It begins with the Individual and the Family. This is the best defense any country can have (plus the citizenry actively and on a daily basis directly participating in the political process, if not for your self-serving laws preventing this aspect).

6. In closing, I make this request—this bullying of our youth must end. NOW. I plead for this with all earnestness and love for every youth and child in Singapore, because I am a father, most of all, and not an overpaid politician or for that matter, a general shielded by a desk. I am not fit to be either of the latter. I am that 99.99 percent (which you clearly abhor) and proud of it. This is how I define myself always—David and Sara's father. Nothing is more glorious than this!

And please be reminded, every child has dreams! It is not for us to take them away from our precious child. David's dreams and human rights were denied him. His manifest diversity was totally ignored! He chose death rather than give up his convictions.

He left us with these written words in an envelope on his bed:

"Do not silence me.

Let my work live."

He ended with this line to me: "Do not fail me again."

I do not plan to.

I leave you with the following:

> "All great truths begin as blasphemies."
>
> —George Bernard Shaw

And

> "If a law is unjust, a man is not only right to disobey it. He is obligated to do so."
>
> —Thomas Jefferson

And this by one of David's favourite philosophers:

> "To learn who rules over you, simply find out who you are not allowed to criticise."
>
> —Voltaire

And the finale. A Poem authored by David. Did you know he left behind a collection of over 50 poems? I thought not. This is just one of them. Please pay special attention to the last 3 lines. We all have much to learn from this brilliant and sensitive child:

Butterfly

Eyes divine like that of a blessed soul,

Etched upon two waves,

Left and Right, raging seas passing

along a shallow shore.

Deceptive and cunning,

Sanguine and dainty,

A dirty dismal beauty hidden in

Vagient flames; Elusive Illusion.

Be it a perplexing mirage or a beam of hope

Sever to pieces, Shards on misty gold—

To kill the illusion, you must kill all hope.

To abandon all pain

You must renounce all gain.

End

—David Cornelius

2015

David desperately wanted to live, going by his papers which he left to me. We all failed him. Most of all, his father for not taking him away. We gave him no choice!

I wrote to you, and then to the PM asking if the buck stopped at your respective desks? Neither replied directly. It was left to a nameless bureaucrat to brush me off. This is the level of respect and compassion we got. Should we have expected more?

I am left to conclude the buck did not stop anywhere in this "rotten state of Denmark," to borrow a phrase from "Hamlet," one of David's favourite plays.

Fear is a tool of our leaders. However, I will stick with what David advised: "Be yourself!"

It is so simple to do.

You, Sir can keep your tool to yourself. I have no use for it.

Thank you.

Yours Truly,

David's father

Please note that in this letter, I stated that with all the military hardware and software the Western Alliance (NATO-East) has in and around Singapore, the island would make for a natural target should the West engage in hostilities in the region with a nonallied country. Any such threat, as I pointed out, would likely emanate from outside Southeast Asia, given that Singapore's immediate neighbors are members of this alliance as well.

After a US B-52 bomber flew over the South China Sea in March of 2019, the defense secretary of the Philippines, Delfin Lorenzana, expressed similar concern; US ships have been traveling the South China Sea, also known as the West Philippine Sea, as part of freedom of navigation exercises, much to the consternation of China, which believes the area belongs to them.

The defense secretary explained that this tension could cause real problems for the Philippines, in that that the Philippines-US Mutual Defense Treaty obligates the countries to come to each other's defense should one of them come under attack. However, it doesn't clarify as to whether disputed territories—including islands in the South China Sea—fall under the auspices of the treaty. Lorenzana stated, "The Philippines is not in a conflict with anyone and will not be at war with anyone in the future. But the United States, with the increased and frequent passage of its naval vessels in the West Philippine Sea, is more likely to be involved in a shooting war. In such a case and on the basis of the MDT, the Philippines would automatically be involved."[19]

It should be apparent to the strategic minds of the military—as it is apparent to me—that the probable outcome in situations like this is not favorable. Namely, it is plausible that a hypersonic nuclear missile strike could be launched on Singapore to wipe out the assets of the Western Alliance, including nuclear carriers and submarines around the island. If hostilities heat up, this is the situation in which we could very well find ourselves. I explained all this to the minister in my letter, lest I be accused of harboring an overly sanguine view of Singapore's defense needs. Quite to the contrary. I understand the potential threats to this nation all too well—but does the defense minister? Do the military strategists? Do all of those who perpetuate the useless tradition of conscription?

If what I've described in the last paragraphs is a legitimate threat—and it is—and if it constitutes the only type of severe threat we face as a nation—which it does—then what is a conscript supposed to do? How are these young men, drafted against their will and despite their individual beliefs and needs, supposed to come between Singaporean citizens and a nuclear missile strike?

This is what I asked the defense minister in my letter. What exactly does Singapore expect of its conscripts? Will it benefit anyone for them to stand out front holding rifles moments before they, like everyone else on the island, are vaporized?

My efforts to bring to light the human rights abuses in Singapore—particularly as they apply to military conscripts—have extended well beyond these open letters, but unfortunately, they

---

19 James Griffiths, "South China Sea: Philippines Warns US Treaty Could Drag It into War Following B-52 Flyover," MSN, March 6, 2019, https://www.msn.com/en-us/news/world/south-china-sea-philippines-warns-us-treaty-could-drag-it-into-war-following-b-52-flyover/ar-BBUpWeC?ocid=spartandhp.

have been answered with the same radio silence. These efforts include visiting the Human Rights Watch (HRW) in San Francisco, where I discussed the dismal outlook for conscientious objectors in Singapore and requested that the HRW shine its powerful light on the situation.

In contrast to my endeavors in Singapore, my visit to the HRW at least netted face-to-face interaction and a sympathetic ear. Still, nothing further has come of it. This ongoing issue, whose ramifications are widespread and drastic, has not received due attention from one of the world's most dedicated human rights organizations.

Following up on the place of conscription in our society, and the many ancillary rights abuses involved in it, is certainly an important aspect of my journey following the loss of my son. However, other matters demand my attention as well. Furthering David's life's work and activism—promoting his legacy—demands that I seek answers for what happened to him from all the institutions that could have contributed to his demise, including his school.

The school wanted to distance itself from our family and our loss. In the weeks following David's passing, and at our constant request, we finally were able to meet two senior officials of the school in the principal's office. In this meeting, two requests were made of the school—first, to hold the memorial service for David in the school's chapel. We had initially made this request nearly a month prior, without any commitment or even reply from the school. The second request, also initially made nearly a month before, was that our family be allowed to sponsor a theater award for the most deserving graduating student, in David's name.

In this meeting, the officials refrained from saying no outright, but one did say this: "We do not want to glorify his death." Sara and I were taken aback by this insulting and insensitive behavior. I thought it was ironic that a huge bust stood in the school's foyer glorifying a known criminal. The bust was there only because the old man's family had created a foundation in his name, through which they donated large sums to the school.

In June 2017, the same month I visited the United States, I sent a letter to the principal assuring that I didn't want to talk about David, exactly; I wanted a chance to discuss the school's curriculum. The letter is reproduced in its entirety below:

Dear Mr. Roberts,

RE: David Cornelius Singh—A Life

It has been over a year. I trust this is long enough in terms of "distance" as you had previously suggested.

I am writing to you to request a meeting. This is not to discuss our initially proposed "Theatre Prize" in honour of David, which clearly the school had no interest.

The meeting is to discuss the curriculum regarding Theatre/Drama and Literature, as taught in the school. I should add this is very important. I do encourage your attendance.

I am available to come by the school anytime which suits you from now until the 1st week of June. Please advise what works for you.

Thank you.

Yours Truly,

David's father

This letter finally earned me a substantive meeting with him. After we'd dispensed with the pleasantries, I launched into what

I had to say. I was not ignorant of the subject matter addressed in many of these classes. As a father who kept up with his son's interests to whatever extent I could—I had seen his books; I was aware of the themes of the plays he acted in; I had observed that his classes would present the cases of various famous individuals who had lost their lives to suicide.

Elsewhere in this book, I detail my own suggestions for helping to prevent suicide in young people. For adults, especially those in instructional and advisory roles, this involves recognizing when young people are being exposed to heavy subject matter that could prove overwhelming at their age and in their often fragile emotional states. When you teach these weighty subjects, you have to remember that your students are still, in many ways, children. You can't introduce books, plays, and history lessons that depict suicide without following up on how these are potentially affecting the students. Through vigorous classroom discussion and through counseling, you have to help these students process what they've learned. You have to help them firmly draw a line between dramatic representation and their own lives, between the admirability of a historical figure's life's work and the way that life ended.

In addition, I made it clear to Mr. Roberts that all of the students had attended public schools previously and thus inherited the issues those schools bestowed upon them. The children SJII was charged with educating and supporting carried with them the anxiety and fear of a public school system that had destroyed their self-confidence and caused enormous emotional and psychological stress. Many of those students had repressed their unpleasant memories for years. But when they arrived at SJII, where the educational system was more interactive and prioritized critical thinking, the repressed memories resurfaced. They could now talk about what they had been through.

But it was up to the school to address those issues—and support their students—directly. Otherwise, the students would be left to grapple with all they had been through alone, which could have dire consequences.

The answer I received at the time *sounded* encouraging. "If we had known then what we know now," I was told, "we could have done something." I was assured that the very matters I'd come there to discuss were at the forefront of the school's measures to prevent further tragedies. The principal told me they had more counselors in place now who knew what to watch out for and would proactively monitor students for troubling behavior.

After the meeting, I sent the following letter, expressing my gratitude for the attitude, as well as my hope that the school would follow through and address the concerns we had discussed.

Dear Mr. Roberts,

RE: David Cornelius Singh—A Life

Thank you and Bro. Lawrence for meeting with Ms. Edna and me in your office on June 01, 2017.

We are gratified by your assurance to actively address the concerns which we expressed during the meeting about a few areas in the practice and study of Theatre and English literature in the School.

We are also encouraged by your advice of the additional action taken by the School since David's passing to assure the safety and protection of every student in the School.

David loved SJII. It was where he found himself. It is the hope of his family that the School continues to promote learning in a passionate way, which David had come to appreciate. David's brilliance was a team effort—the school played a significant part.

While we are disappointed by the manner in which the School had handled its communications with the family since his passing, we feel nevertheless, and in the Spirit of David the Pacifist, that love and mutual understanding are critical to move things forward.

David bequeathed a few of his much-loved collection of books to Mrs. Bull and Mrs. Ng, the teachers he admired, loved and respected the most. They are welcome to the books at their soonest convenience.

Finally, as advised in the meeting, the family plans for David's work and life story to be published. This is in accordance with his last wishes. In this respect, the family may seek the School's support and cooperation in way of allowing us access to his teachers. We trust you will agree to this.

Thank you and best wishes

David's father

In order to get this far, I'd promised that I had no intention of suing; I just wanted to make sure I was being heard. But even with this assurance in place, the reaction I received was extremely circumspect. It was clear to me that teachers and other staff had been discouraged from meeting and/or talking with me. I was made to feel as if David's passing was a mere nuisance. They wanted to put the issue to bed as quickly as possible; they set aside time for me to speak my peace, they nodded when I spoke, and then they ushered me out.

Even David's drama teacher—who had been a shaping influence

in his life and with whom he had been so close—pulled away. She attended his wake but not his memorial service, saying it coincided with a previously planned vacation. She wouldn't support the effort to create a theater award in David's name, although she had initially said she would. I received the clear impression that my reaching out made her uncomfortable.

I am not so removed from the reality of Singaporean youth culture that I believe schools have an easy task. To them falls the unfortunate role of educating kids who are troubled by—and often desperate to escape—a corrupt, oppressive system. In some societies, perhaps incorporating heavier subjects in the school curriculum is not such a threat. But in light of Singapore's omnipresent oppression, it is understandable that death can be recast in young people's minds as an escape.

When schools in Singapore stock their libraries with books that contain suicide scenes, when the main characters in their plays resolve conflict through suicide, when Sylvia Plath's suicide is taught to students alongside her body of work, a deadly issue is too easily romanticized. With the walls of a dim future closing in, Singaporean students are vulnerable to any idea that suggests escape.

My goal is to be on record with all of this. I want my statements, my testimony, and all my challenging questions on the record. I want this because of what David's principal said when I finally met him in person: "If we had known then what we know now, we could have done something."

My ultimate hope is that no other family has to go through what mine has endured—that no parent or sibling has to mourn as we have.

Now they know. It can never again be claimed that the school—or any other institution David was associated with—had no way of understanding what was going on. The school is now officially aware of the warning signs, contributing factors, and dangers to mental health specific to the society in which we live.

My ultimate hope is that no other family has to go through what mine has endured—that no parent or sibling has to mourn as we have.

* * *

David left behind a vast collection of writing—poems, plays, and more—and it is a tentpole of my mission now to see his work published and performed. There is hardly a more appropriate context than this or one of David's most disturbing and powerful poems. In an indictment of the psychiatric system in Singapore and its intersection with conscription, he wrote the following:

WORTHLESS WORDS

For the doctor

I spit a word
And out of its gelatin
Surfaces a blue tin.

Open the lid like a skull
And peer into the portrait
Evergreens. On its shelves are
Cobwebbed cities: wretched things
Ebbing towards a blackholed sky.

On your leather throne, you dissect
Each letter to a pale grey. Outside,
The feathered buildings leap towards
A man on some ledge, who teeters
From the cement canvas to
Your finite night-light.

Dearest doctor,
With your hackneyed complexes
Ancient mathematics
And wandering eyes
Does this widowed window spin
Any webbed white lies?

Always you grope at my latch
Tending to my gardens with
A red stamp and a pack of cigarette-
Wafers the size of my anchors.

Prophet, I dare ask:
Have your callous
Gospels rendered you careless?
While you Command my Spirit and its Disguise
To your willing scalpel,
Oh hear the darkling whispers
It comes chuffing; that black train
Which, when it strikes, will toll
In skids the size of letters on this poem.

It is incumbent upon me to live my life as my son so often urged me to: "Be yourself!" It was his simple but powerful mantra, one he hoped to see all his loved ones adopt and live out, as he did. This is now my life's guiding principle.

I have no interest in labeling myself as an economist, manager, permanent secretary, general, or banker. No. I am now satisfied to say that I am an individual, a human being, living with dignity and without fear. Without a care for the opinion of an elitist and self-serving ruling class.

In a letter to the Singaporean state on April 14, 2017, regarding their broken promise to meet with the family about David's last interview with the armed forces' doctors, I wrote, "Fear is a tool of our leaders. However, I will stick with what David advised: 'Be yourself!' It is so simple to do."

David understood this much more than his father ever did. As a conscientious objector, David had more courage and nobility than any paper general Singapore has ever elevated. David told them about his beliefs, and they did not seem to care.

I will make it my lasting mission to keep delivering my son's message to those who did not listen when he spoke before and to those who never had a chance to hear him. David's loss will not be in vain. His writings, his passions, and his vision for what life could be, as well as his criticism of the institutions that barred the way—all of these things will live on, as David himself lives on.

WALKING IN MY SON'S FOOTSTEPS

The Reporter for Conscience' Sake

The Center on Conscience & War — *Working to extend and defend the rights of Conscientious Objectors to war since 1940*

Volume 75   Summer/Fall 2018   Number 1

A History of the Selective Service System Violating the Rights of Conscience
Bill Galvin, Counseling Coordinator, with CCW Staff

During the Vietnam War, it was the draft that enabled the country to prolong a war that had long been opposed by the majority of the people. The draft was the focus of many anti-war actions. Finally, in 1973, after 33 years of an active draft, the government ended conscription. On April 1, 1975, Selective Service registration was ended, and the entire system was put into 'deep standby.'

In 1980, President Jimmy Carter brought Selective Service out of standby and resumed registration. The Soviet Union had just invaded Afghanistan, and President Carter wanted to 'send a message' that the US could be ready for war at any time.

In the 38 years since registration resumed, no one has been drafted. During that period, besides registering young men, Selective Service has developed and maintained plans for how a draft might work if it were to resume, including training draft board members around the country and maintaining an alternative service program for conscientious objectors.

They've also kept busy instituting increasingly repressive and invasive ways to coerce people to register.

All male citizens and residents of the US (regardless of documentation or status) are required to register during a 60-day period that begins 30 days before their 18th birthday. The vast majority of men have violated this law by not registering during that window of time. Selective Service happily accepts registrations that are made even years later, but they will not accept registrations from individuals after they turn 26.

Back in 1980, some of those required to register had older brothers who had been drafted during the Vietnam War, and the memory of that war was still very much a part of the public consciousness. Selective Service acknowledged that hundreds of thousands of young men had failed to register during the first year of registration. A significant anti-draft organization formed – CARD, the Committee Against Registration and the Draft, which had chapters throughout the country and organized anti-draft conferences. There were anti-draft marches in Washington, DC and elsewhere around the country. On October 12, 1982, sixty people were arrested for civil disobedience, blocking the entrance at the Selective Service headquarters in Washington, DC.

The government decided to prosecute a handful of resisters, expecting that the publicity would scare others into registering. Instead, the prosecutions had the opposite effect: the defendants became part of the national conversation and were on the evening news, with some describing their resistance to participating with Selective Service as answering to a 'higher law;' others questioned the legitimacy of maintaining the apparatus of a military draft in a free and democratic society. Their witness inspired others to make their own, and non-compliance with registration actually increased in those communities where people were prosecuted.

In response, starting in 1982, the government developed other ways to coerce people to register, known at time as "Solomon Laws," named after the member of Congress who first introduced them. The first such effort was to link draft registration with federal financial aid. In order to receive Pell Grants, college work/study, loans, or other federal financial assistance for education, one has to verify either that they are indeed registered with Selective Service or that they are not required to register. In solidarity with men's resistance, some women refused to help the government enforce the law by verifying that they were not required to register. As a result, those women also were denied federal financial aid.

Next, the government linked federal job training programs to draft registration and made registration a prerequisite for

History, continued on page 4

Also Inside: Torture and Triumph of WWI COs Shown in US Premiere of *This Evil Thing*..page 3

David's Story: Protections for COs Save Lives...page 6

This issue of *The Reporter* carries a tribute to David on page 6, titled *David's story: Protections for COs Save Lives*.

154

CHAPTER 8

Brainwashing a Nation: How Singapore's Culture Hurts Children and Families

THIEF

"That is wanting a good deal, of course, when you have to trample upon the lives, the hearts, the prejudices of others—but no matter—I shouldn't want to trample upon the little lives."
—Edna Pontellier in Kate Chopin's The Awakening

Floundering about in the dead-sea
He curled, like a fetus-
Torn from the womb
By His bloodied hands that beat in rhythms
Of madness and torment.

Foolishly waiting-
Wallowing in the white.
Then in one hot flush of red
Came the gush, the malignant ray
Rushing in torrents, drowning love's toy.

And now you want more
Clawing for the remains of skin
A thrust, a push, as the air wears thin-
Strangling; the snake coils like a noose
Spoiling the scents of sense and spleen.

And that frenzied cracking of joints
Blood and Bone you snapped like twigs
Brain burst open and burned within
Heart tossed in heat upon witch figs;

Yet you left his soul intact.

Like a treasure on lost shore,
You pulled it by its chains in clutter
Back to the cold of clean-clammed hands
As the boys you bore long before
Whilst your shuttered chilled lips dare mutter
That curse that stole our firefly days.

—David C. Singh, ca. 2015

Singapore is called free now—an independent nation. But this claim is far from true; the predominant culture in Singapore today is one of brainwashing. With the help of the armed forces, psychiatric system, and public schools, the government compels young people to give up their freedom bit by bit in the name of patriotism, pledging loyalty to a nation and regime that demonstrate little concern for their welfare.

Didn't we notice that after 1965, when we gained our so-called independence, the colonial laws remained? And to this day, it is the same. We enjoy no freedom of press, no open electoral system, no antidiscrimination laws. The secret police are endowed with unlimited powers, and trials in court are not a necessary precondition for indefinite detention. Per section 377A of the penal code, which criminalizes gay relationships, gay couples are denied public housing—meaning they subsidize others through their tax dollars without being able to reap any similar benefits.

The police are given these unrestrained powers through the Internal Security Act and the Criminal Law Act, laws enacted by the colonial administration long before independence. They allow the colonial administration to detain anyone indefinitely and without due process. These laws remain and have been strengthened. At least the colonials had jury trials in capital cases of murder. After independence, the jury system was removed. The excuse given was that the jurors could be swayed by emotional appeal from defendants. That's rubbish. I contend that the real reason is to keep people out of governance—to prevent them from holding the state accountable.

Singapore is a city in the Malay Sea pretending to be a country. The city's British colonizers designed it to be an oligarchic enterprise—and I hold that it remains one today. We have oligarchic corporations that face minimal competition and are subsidized by the people. Racist policies prevent deserving ethnic Malay citizens from serving in senior and strategic positions in the armed forces.[20]

---

20 Shiwen Yap, "Unfair Discrimination of Malays in National Service," *The Online*

A classist stratification in public schools does a severe disservice to droves of students every year.

People are cowed into accepting that all of this—the dearth of protection for our individual rights, the invasions of our privacy, our unequal protection under the law—not only can't be fought, but is incompatible with the concept of freedom. As long as the government insists that the name for our shared experience in this country is liberty, as long as we obediently accept that message as the truth, we will accept anything and everything else they want us to.

As long as the government insists that the name for our shared experience in this country is liberty, as long as we obediently accept that message as the truth, we will accept anything and everything else they want us to.

Singapore's fifty-plus-year-old forced military service program (National Service) is the worst offender. Its continued existence is an affront to our free will and autonomy, one that too many of us are brainwashed into accepting without question. The proper time for its dissolution came and passed long ago; between suicides and other fatalities, it has claimed too many victims already—including my son, David. The ministry of defense refuses to release the figures regarding this, ignoring my October 2017 request (which I share in the previous chapter). This is the level of respect we receive as citizens.

Despite its name, conscription, or National Service, has never been about Singapore's defense. It was created to produce a brainwashed youth, marching goose-stepped to the tune of an elitist ruling class. David knew this, and this is why he opposed it to the end. Let

---

Citizen, January 30, 2012, https://www.theonlinecitizen.com/2012/01/30/unfair-discrimination-of-malays-in-national-service/.

me be clear on this point:

A purpose of basic training is brainwashing.

Military personnel have heard it said that basic training is brainwashing, and many tend to dismiss this accusation as subjective liberal propaganda.[21] It's neither subjective nor propaganda. It's an established fact. Professor Margaret Singer summarized brainwashing.

> Coercive psychological systems are behavioral change programs which use psychological force in a coercive way to cause the learning and adoption of an ideology or designated set of beliefs, ideas, attitudes, or behaviors. The essential strategy used by the operators of these programs is to systematically select, sequence, and coordinate many different types of coercive influence, anxiety, and stress-producing tactics over continuous periods of time. [22]

Singapore's defense had been and continues to be guaranteed by its creators—"former" colonial owners, Britain, the United States, and NATO-East. These folks operate military facilities on the island, which they still own, along with the descendants of the comprador class who helped the British East India Company (EIC)—a private, for-profit corporation—invade and occupy Singapore in 1819.

Sir Thomas Raffles, an employee of the EIC, was their point man. His statue stands today by the Singaporean riverside, pompously reminding all of us that we are not and never have been an indepen-

---

21 Former minister of interior and defense Dr. Goh Kend Swee, however, acknowledged according to the CIA that "the reserve training program is more sociological than military, and is intended mainly to produce a 'closely-knit community'" ("Weekly Summary Special Report: Singapore on the Eve of Lee Kuan Yew's Visit to the US," Directorate of Intelligence no. 45, October 6, 1967).

22 Margaret Thaler Singer, PhD, "Coercive Mind Control Tactics," Psychological Harassment Information Association, accessed June 20, 2018, http://www.psychologicalharassment.com/coercive-mind-control-tactics.htm.

dent entity. You would think that an independent country would see to it immediately after independence that this statue of our colonizer was removed and discarded.

* * *

When Indonesians bravely fought and gained their independence from the Dutch in 1945, the colonials and their comprador class were duly concerned. Sukarno, the socionationalist leader of that struggle, was removed twenty years later in a military coup that installed General Suharto as president and that led to a violent pacification campaign in which hundreds of thousands of Indonesians were murdered by organized criminal elements. Historians have judged this to be one of the most horrendous massacres in modern history.[23]

What the Indonesian people were left with was a military dictatorship that accelerated the exploitation of the country's resources over the next thirty years. Many of these ill-gotten and bloody proceeds were invested or deposited in Singapore. The funds were then reinvested—*laundered* is the word some would use—in real estate on the island.

Over the two centuries since its "creation" by the EIC, Singapore attracted the proceeds of the legal and illegal trade in the Malay archipelagos' produce. The banking and insurance companies that came about were EIC- and comprador-owned and controlled. To put

---

23 Geoffrey B. Robinson, *The Killing Season: A History of the Indonesian Massacres, 1955–66* (New Jersey: Princeton University Press, 2018).

it mildly, Singapore was—and is—a tax haven.[24], [25], [26]

Singapore's economic prosperity had little to do with the "foresight" of a dictator, as school textbooks teach our children. It had more to do with centralizing the colonial exploitation of the region. This, then, is what our national service conscripts are supposed to *defend*.

This means of "defense," desired and engineered by the elites, hinges not on military fortification, but on a population willing to submit to everlasting control and exploitation. Military conscription serves that purpose.

Yet we pretend we are an independent country with an armed force that could contend with those we've been exploiting for two hundred years now—the Malaysians and Indonesians. But we need to wake up. The same NATO that controls us also controls the seas, along with the armaments and fuel supplies to countries of this region. No one is invading anyone else without their participation and leadership.

Take the United Nations Treaty for the Prohibitions of Nuclear weapons. On July 7, 2017, the United Nations General Assembly (UNGA) voted on the treaty. One hundred and twenty-two countries voted for it, one country voted against it, and only one—Singapore—abstained. Every other country in Southeast Asia—

---

24 "Indonesians declare 117.3t rupiah of Singapore Assets Under Tax Amnesty," *Business Times*, September 16, 2016, https://www.businesstimes.com.sg/government-economy/indonesians-declare-1173t-rupiah-of-singapore-assets-under-tax-amnesty.

25 Sara Webb, "Private Banking: Singapore, Indonesia in Private Banking Tug-of-War," *Euromoney*, September 11, 2015, https://www.euromoney.com/article/b12klwdwr8p81p/private-banking-singapore-indonesia-in-private-banking-tugofwar.

26 "Singapore is World's Fifth-largest Tax Haven, behind HK: Report," *Today*, January 31, 2018, https://www.todayonline.com/singapore/singapore-worlds-fifth-largest-tax-haven-behind-hk-report.

including Malaysia, Indonesia, Thailand, and the Philippines—voted in favor of it.

Shortly after, I wrote a letter to Singapore's foreign ministry requesting an explanation, since UNGA's action was not mentioned on the ministry's website. I received a lengthy reply explaining the Singaporean government's position. In a nutshell, they said they could not support the treaty due to their belief that the treaty "should be consistent with other international agreements, such as the treaties establishing nuclear weapons-free zones, the Treaty on the Non-Proliferation of Nuclear Weapons, and the UN Convention on the Law of the Sea."

They also felt more time was needed since "certain provisions were not framed as well as they might, thereby giving rise to legal uncertainty with regard to the implications on the rights and obligations of States Parties under other important treaties."

It is clear to me that the Singaporean government's decision rested on the undeniable fact that the country is a NATO-East base of operations, with its attendant nuclear-armed warships, submarines, and aircrafts.

Years from now, our children and grandchildren—with the advantage of hindsight—will see how untenable the decision to abstain had been. The pertinent question then will be: Why were the people of Singapore silent about this?

This ill-advised decision to abstain was a major blunder in Singapore's international relations, giving the impression that the country is not truly independent. Years from now, our children and grandchildren—with the advantage of hindsight—will see how untenable the decision to abstain had been. The pertinent question then will be: *Why were the people of Singapore silent about this?* My reply, as always, is that we only have ourselves to blame by placing our lives and trust in the hands of unelected bureaucrats and undemocratic rulers. Both are, in the final analysis, not accountable to We the People.

That said, there should be a simple and logical choice for those who genuinely believe Singapore needs defending. That choice is to enlist in the regular armed forces of their own volition. We don't need National Service! The fear that we would have no protection without it is unfounded.

When we look at the issue in its full context, it's easy to see that military conscription is not about national defense. It also becomes easier to see what it *is* about. I wasted two and a half years of my youth in the armed forces, and after that, they asked if I wanted to sign on permanently! I can only guess that I must have appeared effectively brainwashed for them to ask.

* * *

National Service is the ultimate example of pervasive, countrywide brainwashing, but you can see this occurring in many other ways as well. Singapore operates as a well-oiled machine—all of its pieces work together to keep the population as docile as possible.

The public school system in Singapore, for instance, is not designed to promote creativity. It is a system for classifying and separating children, starting in third grade, based on their performance on standardized tests and curricula. Nothing crushes a child's confidence more effectively than an education system that puts a premium on uniformity and rote regurgitation.

This process additionally creates extreme anxiety among Singaporean school children; from a young age, they feel the pressure to compete for slots in the elite public schools. Typically they are dispatched from school each day with a staggering amount of homework due the following day. They are robbed of time to unwind and simply be children afterward: it's an effective process if the goal is molding and controlling minds.

In fact, the vision of the Ministry of Education is summarized in its slogan since 1997: "Thinking Schools, Learning Nation" (TSLN). The ministry's website proudly proclaims its mission to "mould the future of the nation by moulding the people who will determine the future of the nation."[27]

In our family, we watched the negative impacts of this play out in David. While Sara was doing well in high school, David was considered an average student in primary school—even though it was evident to all who knew him that he was an exceptionally bright boy. David was extremely individualistic, which made it quite impossible for him to conform; as a consequence, he tuned out of the system. The public education system doesn't merely fail to reward independent thinkers; it has no tolerance for them. It works to neutralize them.

I have never subscribed to the idea that there are "dumb" kids, as the classification and stratification system in Singapore would lead one to believe. What I do believe is that parents, teachers, and educational systems can fail young, receptive minds. This seems to occur most frequently as a result of a failure to directly engage the child.

I remember watching a documentary on TV some years ago about a teacher in China who went to the home of each and every student she taught to meet the guardians and siblings. In due time, she made herself a team member in the life of each child. How moved her students must have been by this demonstration of true caring and

---

[27] See the ministry's website at https://www.moe.gov.sg/about.

passion.

There are good teachers everywhere. Their good efforts are undermined, however, when the education system they work within—and moreover, the culture as a whole—undermines their efforts. The system does not have much room for empathetic teachers who wish to cultivate creative thinking.

In Singapore there is an additional reason for the stratification of our public schools, and hence our children—the connection between the ministries or departments of education and manpower. Being a statist system, the manpower ministry develops long-term projections for the city's specific labor needs. The education ministry then works on that basis, culling each year's cohort as necessary for their plans—students who don't do well in the standardized tests are denied access to higher public education. Those who can afford to do so leave for the West (usually America, Australia, or the UK) to attend reputable colleges and universities, which readily accept them.

> *There are good teachers everywhere. Their good efforts are undermined, however, when the education system they work within—and moreover, the culture as a whole—undermines their efforts.*

Educators—by which I mean anyone or any group that supports a child's education—who blame a child for their failure to move up the formal education chain should reflect carefully on their own shortcomings. We all could learn from that special teacher in China. She did not lose faith in any of her students; seeing the need for a more personalized approach, she did something about it.

Our children's future is planned by the unelected and faceless bureaucrats in the ministries of education and labor. They decide who goes on to university in Singapore, because Singapore offers few public universities—unlike in the West, where every country has hundreds of them. And in those few, admission is purposefully restricted. While in the West, higher education is a right, in Singapore it is a privilege—higher-level education is rationed!

By 2012, when Sara had graduated from junior college and enrolled in a university in Australia, David was also making great progress in his schoolwork after he left the public education system and entered an international school. The kids had many friends and were deeply focused on school and social life. As a parent, I could not have asked for anything more than this. But it is a testament to the intelligence, resilience, and determination of my children that they rose to such heights in their education—they were certainly not aided in this by the public school system. It could even be said that they had to work to recover the self-confidence they lost during their public school years.

When we moved David to his private high school, he became an excellent student, scoring distinctions in every subject in the final year, 2015. He was so happy: he would scream in ecstasy when he found out he had aced a project or test, and he would rush to inform me.

The only obstacle to his ambitions, he felt, was his impending two-year military conscription. For someone like David—a pacifist, a conscientious objector, and ultimately a thinker—this meant going back into a system he hated, one that had given up on him long ago. He had recognized this system in his public school years, and he understood that military conscription was another moving part in the same machine. It was a past he had put behind him but would have to relive again soon. This fear was topmost in his mind.

Any education system that deliberately stunts a student's progress is a corrupt system that will never benefit the citizens. David knew that. From his perspective, his parents' separation and the public school system in Singapore were two coinciding traumatic events in his life. He was doing the psychologically healthy thing by trying to move beyond these traumas and afford himself time to heal, but the state laid claim to him once more in the form of the military draft. He was never going to trade in his newly emancipated identity for the old, broken, and repressed one.

He made his choice, if ever he had one.

* * *

Singapore was a creation of the British Crown, and it continues to be a strategic asset to them and to the Singaporean government—but sadly, not to the families of Singapore, particularly the children. For example, the grounds of the presidential palace in tiny Singapore—a city-state at 719 square kilometers—take up a whopping one hundred acres, whereas the White House in Washington, DC, occupies a mere eighteen of them.[28] Still, the state regularly seizes lands for public works and condos, offering the rationale that the country is short of land. And when you begin to really look behind the existing infrastructure, you find a system of laws (and law enforcement) that confines a population within a politicogeographical boundary, with the notion that the people materially benefit from this unique confinement. It is called a social contract.

In exchange for this so-called beneficence from the state, people sacrifice liberty. They allow themselves to be socialized, pacified, and

---

28 "The Istana," National Library Board Singapore, accessed May 14, 2019, http://eresources.nlb.gov.sg/infopedia/articles/SIP_807_2005-02-01.html.

programmed to create a uniform identity—an identity that is distinct from that of people in another geographical area or state only on the surface. In academic parlance, it is the process of political socialization. In layman's terms, it's mind control.

As one can imagine, a political agenda so endorsed and embedded works its way into every part of a culture. While it begins in earnest with schoolchildren, it continues when those children are grown—and can be of even more use to the state. When we reach maturity in Singapore, we are ready to take on jobs that will consume our waking hours in the same way schoolwork did in our youth, leaving us little time or energy to object to the way things are going or really to think beyond day-to-day life at all.

We work long hours to afford the necessities—a home, a car, educational expenses—which in Singapore come with a crippling price tag: it has some of the highest real estate prices and car taxes in the world. The average two-bedroom apartment costs in excess of USD$1.2 million. A Toyota Camry, which costs about $24,000 in the United States, clocks in at more than $160,000 in Singapore![29] On top of this stress, parents are impelled to join the school system in its campaign to make young students excel, to make them *competitive*. When children do not perform as well as the Singaporean education system thinks they should, their parents are guilted into pushing them harder at home. In other words, parents become agents of this system of mind and behavioral control.

What I've described is ordinary life for the adult citizens of Singapore, who wish nothing more than to have careers and establish families. It is a life I left behind. A life I had no control over—work

---

29 Toyota Passenger Car Price," Toyota Inchcape Singapore, accessed May 14, 2019, https://www.toyota.com.sg/finance/pricelist-passenger?gclid=EAlalQobChMl1d24rb_q4AlVww0rCh3LdAGjEAAYASABEgJw3vD_BwE.

that did not bring me happiness or satisfaction. For thirty years, I worked at a feverish pace at a job I disliked in order to make money to pay basic bills and put my children through school. This was the way society is organized. Even when someone buys a home and celebrates that major milestone, the reality is that most people will be slaving for the publicly subsidized monopoly bankers for twenty-five years to pay off the mortgage.

For years, I cooperated with the system in Singapore, working without giving a thought to the way every one of us, especially our children, is damaged from this. The kids had not asked for this way of living, however, and it was becoming as evident to them as to any astute observer that Singapore's system is not one of individuals—here we are all digits. Our current prime minister, Lee Hsien Loong, is the son of Lee Kuan Yew, the first prime minister, who ruled for thirty years. Even when his son took over, Lee Kuan Yew continued to rule from behind the scenes, serving as senior minister for his successor, Goh Chok Tong, and as minister mentor to his son until 2011. He was not shy about his oppressive beliefs, once stating, "Between being loved and feared, I have always believed Machiavelli was right. If nobody is afraid of me, I'm meaningless."[30] This is the mentality of a bully, and it's a culture he engendered to this day, through his son and others.

* * *

The Hollywood comedian and actor Groucho Marx said, "Military intelligence is a contradiction in terms." My son knew this was true,

---

30 "Lee Kuan Yew: His Most Memorable Quotes," *The Telegraph*, March 23, 2015, https://www.telegraph.co.uk/news/worldnews/asia/singapore/11489177/Lee-Kuan-Yew-his-most-memorable-quotes.html.

especially with regard to *forced military service*. He understood keenly that military conscription was not about the defense of the nation—and he could never stand for what it truly *was* about. He understood that conscription was about nothing more than the subordination of the individual to the state, and this knowledge caused him tremendous dread and depression. It is this thought that leads me to another realm in which Singapore—as a nation, as a culture—fails its citizens.

Military psychiatrists are presented to us as objective medical professionals who prioritize the mental health and overall welfare of their patients. I have extensively addressed psychiatry as a whole in a separate chapter; here I want to focus on how it fits into this comprehensive system of brainwashing. And there is no one better to explain that relationship in convincing detail than David.

I have chosen to share a section from the many writings David left me, this part reflecting his interviews with the military psychiatrist. It is extremely painful for me to read these words and to share them, but I believe it is critical to an understanding of just how dismissive the Singaporean government is of human individuality and human needs.

The government presents itself as caring, or at least responsible, but nothing could be further from the truth. Charged with evaluating the fragile emotional condition of a young man with endless talent and great ambition, they instead wrote off his cries for help, ignoring the evidence of how endangered his mental health had become. They used their sessions with him to repackage National Service as the answer to all of his concerns. In other words, they did precisely what the Singaporean government is known for: they used their resources and authority to attempt to brainwash a struggling but brilliant young man who should have been able to trust them.

This writing is structured as a back-and-forth exchange between my son and the military's psychiatrist.

- You take everything.

- What do you mean

- You empty my soul

- I don't understand

- You make me bleed.

- You need help, let us help you

- Please leave me alone

- You have no choice

- Please leave me alone

- You must come with us. You belong here.

- I do not belong to you

- This is your duty—you must protect this homeland

- Why don't you?

- Who will lead this country when it is led to ruin?

- You have already led it to ruin, you who spit venom in the slits of your teeth. How do you—how can you doom boys to a lifetime of death without ever tasting it?

- Are you a man?

- You who whisper lies like scalding mist.

- You will love it when it is all over.

- You cannot know what love is. You steal boys and shape them into your version of men.

- We teach them to be independent

- Bullshit. You are all murderers.

- There is no war.

- Mass slaughter of the human identity. You crush their freedom and keep us on a leash like dogs the instant we are conceived. Generations of youth compressed to dust.

- Watch your tongue.

- I can never run away.

- You cannot run away.

- This soul now aches for lives stolen and youths burnt up in your cruel conflagration. Men go in with opinions and leave sharing only yours.

- We will have you jailed up.

- Jail the fool who speaks of suicide. Kill me for all I care. Let me die so I can leave this pile of shit. This world is a crumbling pile of garbage where a few men own everything and the rest, nothing. You enslave and you take, and you gorge. But one day you will die and you will lie in the ashes of your former "glory," gripped with an all-consuming fear of having ruined countless lives and drowned empowered personalities.

- That's it.

- That's it.

- That's it.

- Kill me

- Kill me

- Kill

- Me

- Please

-

On a recent visit to the United States, I was able to visit MIT, Harvard, and Boston University. I could not help thinking of how strongly my son would have approved of my visit. He was always learning, and these institutions were among those he most admired.

As I walked on the campuses, I felt how it would have been for him if he were a student here. The happiness and liberation he would have felt just walking around. But he knew of this feeling. He felt it when he, Sara, and I visited NYU in 2012 and then again when he and I returned in 2014. It was his dream to live in New York, or at least somewhere in America, where he could be free to pursue his passion, uninterrupted and in earnest, without fear or censure.

Where being gay is not a crime. Where freedom begins with the individual, not the state. Where free speech is not a rebellious act. Where learning is limitless, academic freedom is taken seriously, and you are encouraged as an individual—to repeat my son's most-used

He is my inspiration as I fight to expose the culture and government of Singapore as the self-serving institutions they are, forces that have damaged many bright young individuals—and will damage many more unless we do something about it.

phrase—to "be yourself!"

My son has taught me so many lessons. He grew up steeped in the same system of mind control that affects all of Singapore's children, but he never allowed it to defeat him. He is my inspiration as I fight to expose the culture and government of Singapore as the self-serving institutions they are, forces that have damaged many bright young individuals—and will damage many more unless we do something about it.

CHAPTER 9

How to Help a Teen Who May Be Suicidal—Advice for Friends, Parents, and Educators

---

14/2/2017

Dear David,

Marking today, it's been a year since you've been gone. I'm still annoyed at the fact you chose Valentine's Day to leave—yes, I'm sure it must have been a symbolic date and all that jazz. Congrats, you've ruined Valentine's Day for me, though I'm sure that must have been your plan. I'm sure that one day, I'll realize what you meant by leaving on this day. It's weird with you gone. Life has stayed the same. When you left, I thought I wouldn't be able to move on, I didn't want to leave you behind.

I remember the day I found out about your death. I found out through WhatsApp whilst at work (yes, I chose to work on Valentine's because I needed that cash), and just stared at my phone in disbelief, thinking it was a joke. My body reacted faster than my brain did, my hands started shaking and my eyes started to well up. It came to a point where I couldn't see in front of me because my eyes were filled with tears, and I had to leave work immediately. I sat in the taxi, on the way to Kimi's house, crying. I couldn't think. The taxi driver asked me why I was crying, and I told him what happened. He started talking about how now children were so spoilt, fragile, and weak, and that God would take care of you. I remember getting so angry because I knew you chose not to believe in God, and you definitely were not weak.

I saw Kimi and started crying again. We were so angry. So angry that you left us without saying bye. So angry that you didn't call us for help. So angry that you didn't think we were worthy enough of being of any help to you. We were your friends!

During the night wakes, your dad placed a book where we could write all our wishes to you. I'm sure he meant well, but I wrote one of the nastiest messages in my life then. It was filled with swear words and curses, reflecting my anger and hurt.

Your funeral was only five days away, and I had volunteered to give a speech. I declined at first, thinking that it's best to let those closest to you speak. I didn't want to overestimate my value as a friend over your family. When I heard that only your sister was speaking, I decided to grab hold of my emotions and do this for you.

I'll tell you this now, my speech at your funeral was terrible. I had a few days to prepare, I was still furious at you, and I was expected to say good things about you. It was presented horribly as well, I was snuffling and crying in the middle—urghh I wasn't proud of it.

I'm sorry. I know you probably wanted an amazing speech filled with literary devices and all, but I didn't manage to do it.

I tried hard with the speech at your first memorial though, and I think I redeemed myself. You know I'm not a very good writer (you've said it before). I'm more of a science geek, but I gave it my best shot. I made a plan, I structured it, backed my claims about you with evidence, and focused it on what I could talk about—you being an amazing friend and inspiration for me. It's not the best speech (Sara's is—your sister is a literature genius who understood you so well) but I'm proud of it.

And I hope you're proud of it too.

What I didn't dare to talk about was my emotions about you. About you telling me countless times you wanted to kill yourself, when you were sober or drunk. About you telling me you've been crying because the world is unjust. I didn't dare talk about the scars and cuts that started appearing on your arms and legs—which happened years ago. I remember once you were talking about killing yourself to me and Kimi, and she was trying to argue with you. But I've heard you tell me that so many times—it's like I've become immune to it. I didn't bother fighting back this time. I gave up. I'm not sure if I gave up on you before you gave up on me.

I remember another time when you told me that Kat accused you of being selfish if you died and left us behind. You asked me what I thought. I said I'd feel sad but I'd understand. I lied. I don't understand why you chose to leave. I still feel that you're the selfish one for hurting us. But then again, you might be in more pain living here in our world. But I wouldn't know, because you hide it too damn well.

When you started cutting, I remember grabbing your hand and asking you what the hell did you think you were doing. You said you didn't want to talk about it at first, but eventually I pried it out of you. I didn't know if I should tell someone—you made it sound like you were handling it fine. Since you made your cuts on your arms, exposed to the world, I assumed you wanted people to notice it. Because I assumed other people would notice it and do something about it, I didn't do anything. But, no one did anything. Not even our teachers. A while after, you said you started seeing the psychiatrist and I assumed you'd be fine. Though I was aware of the fact that you thought your psychiatrist didn't understand you and was useless. I could blame it on the fact that I didn't know how to help, that I didn't know what to do.

But I can't.

It's my fault for being a horrible friend and not doing anything. I understood you well, we had many in-depth conversations, but I would shy away whenever you talked about death—I would make it a rational argument, not an emotional one. I tried to un-personalize the situation. Yet being one of the people who could understand you (at least a bit—I hope so), I didn't do anything. I gave up on you. I'm sorry. I'm so sorry. When your dad and sister thank me for being such a great friend to you, my hatred and disgust towards myself grows.

Like I said in the beginning, life has gone forwards and yet stayed the same. I'm doing fine, I can laugh and have fun. I remember thinking once to myself: Why aren't you affected more? Why aren't you crying more? Is it because you didn't really love David?

But then, there are times when I'm on Facebook reading the news about refugees, the Orlando bombings, human rights, etc. That's what gets me. I was doing homework one night, and suddenly I thought of you and just started crying. Tears continued to fall to the point where I couldn't contain my tears and had to stop work. I hugged my knees to sleep that night.

The next morning, I'm fine. It's like nothing ever happened.

I hate myself for being okay without you. I hate myself for not starting to read the books you've left behind for me. It's like I just don't want to remember you—like I just want to keep you in the past, and I don't want to figure out why you left. You're just, gone.

There was one night, I remember finally sharing with my parents that you had talked to me about taking your life countless times, and my mother asked me:

"Why didn't you do anything?"

My dad proceeded to shout at me, telling me I was the most selfish person on Earth.

I don't talk to my family about you anymore.

That stung. It still stings. But it deserves to sting. Because it's true. I'm a horrible friend.

You would think that has changed me. But nope. I've met friends here in the UK that have told me they were depressed. I don't know if they really mean it or if they're trying to get attention (because I'm not that close to them) but just as always, I say nothing. I can't do it again, David. I can't go through the fights I had with you, with someone else. I don't want to get close to someone with these suicidal thoughts because I don't think I can take it. I don't want to give up on a friend again so I don't want to have friends. I don't want to be responsible for their death.

So really, I'm the selfish one.

I don't know if I'll ever have the guts to tell this to your dad or anyone else. They might not say it, but they'd probably hate me for life. I'd hate me too. So I'm writing it down. So I won't forget. I'm the coward, the selfish one. I'm a horrible friend.

I'm sorry.

In this chapter, I include letters from David's dear friend Liz—which I know had to be enormously painful for her to write and share—with her permission and with gratitude to her. None of us hate Liz or blame her, as she fears. Certainly it is painful to think of David expressing his demons and none of his loved ones being able to redirect his course, but depression—particularly teenage depression—is difficult for loved ones to deal with.

While there were complex reasons for David's depression—reasons related to the stifling society in which he lived and the principles that governed his world—depression itself and many of the same behaviors he exhibited leading up to his suicide are frequently seen in young people. It is difficult enough for parents and others in positions of authority to know just what should be done to help a vulnerable young person navigate these treacherous waters; for their peers, the task can seem hopelessly daunting.

In this chapter, I want to share some insights on the preventable—and mendable—factors that can contribute to a teenager's suicidal ideation, including bullying and its modern cousin, cyberbullying. I also wish to emphasize the importance of speaking up.

Often teenagers feel they are being put in an impossible position when a friend talks about taking their own life. Sometimes the matter may seem to dissipate altogether after a discussion and after they resume their regular routine. I believe that sometimes, as well, it simply does not seem real. When we cannot fathom a loved one being gone from our lives, it is difficult to wrap our heads around the possibility that they could ever follow through on a threat to take their life.

It could be that there's a problem in how we, in broader society, tend to portray the teenage years. Clearly these are years that flood with new, exciting experiences; between the forward momentum from childhood into adulthood and the constant shifting of hormones, it is also true that this can be a time of some drama. Of exaggerating and overstating things, of caring intensely about something one moment only to lose interest in it the next. All of this is normal enough and fine to discuss, but I believe there's another important angle to adolescence that would benefit from wider acknowledgement.

Even though teenagers still—wonderfully—tend to retain a childlike resilience and lightheartedness during these years when they also have one foot firmly planted in the adult world. As they are shrieking and gossiping and giggling about crushes, as they are worried about what to wear and what kind of image they have in school, as they hop between moods, they also see the future moving rapidly toward them.

In school—and this is especially the case for those studious pupils who invest themselves in timeless dramatic books and plays—they are exposed to ideas that do not fit tidily into their teenage world. In history class, they learn of wars, of the savagery and brutality that have always largely defined the nation-making. In civics and in the surrounding world, they are exposed to grave political matters. In literature and in theater, they wade into stories that depict adult characters who become despondent, or who valiantly object to something taking place in the world of the story, and some of these characters take their own lives in protest.

It is my belief that the dismissive way many adults talk about teenagers—and about the concerns specific to their lives in this era—is unfair. It fails to acknowledge the weighty matters related to their future, their principles, and the emotions they are grappling with. I fear that it is dangerous to treat all teenagers' concerns like dramatic whims that will pass. If adults do not establish an atmosphere of respect for young people's serious challenges, how are these young people supposed to effectively deal with their own obstacles—or their friends'?

> *It is my belief that the dismissive way many adults talk about teenagers—and about the concerns specific to their lives in this era—is unfair. It fails to acknowledge the weighty matters related to their future, their principles, and the emotions they are grappling with.*

It occurs to me as well that there needs to be greater contextualization in schools of some of the heavy and potentially disturbing ideas that teens are exposed to. While they are no longer children—and in that regard are well on their way to becoming independent thinkers—they are not yet adults. A teenager still lacks an adult's capacity for weighing serious information calmly, for distancing themselves from it enough to look at it objectively.

I believe it is incumbent upon educators who introduce topics that involve great violence, depression, suicide, and so forth to hold discussions with the students afterward in which they examine these elements outside the context of the story or history book. The views of the students should be listened to and further discussed within the class, as means of sharing their unique and yet, in some situations, shared experiences.

It could also help students who are reading the works of, for instance, Sylvia Plath, to calmly and rationally discuss her suicide in a way that offers an objective assessment, if it is at all possible. They could speak of what talent was taken from the world and of what else she might have gone on to create. They could speak empathetically, certainly—expressing sorrow for a woman so disturbed that she would end her life—and at the same time talking about what could have been done to prevent this ending. What family members and friends could have done to intervene. What signs she may have exhibited, and how loved ones could have reacted.

* * *

It seems that all of us go through depression sometimes. It can well up when someone has long been contending with anger and sadness, and it can strike at any age. It makes sense that this condition is especially likely to affect teenagers, who are often balancing pressures from every front—family, friends, school, and so forth. When the weight of hopelessness does not lift after the usual efforts have been made to cheer them up, it can worsen and can become a serious threat.

It is important that young people understand that suicide is a real threat when depression has hold of them or one of their friends. A problematic belief has gained traction in our culture that if someone talks about committing suicide, they are unlikely to go through with it. This may stem from the wider belief that nothing you're able to talk about can truly be that bad. Whatever the case may be, it is critical that young people understand that this a myth—*it is not true.*

There are several warning signs of suicidal thoughts; they do not apply to one and all, of course, but it can be very helpful to watch for

these signals, and to act promptly if these things are observed:
- Talking about committing suicide
- Discussing persistent hopeless or guilty feelings
- Easily losing concentration or being unable to think clearly
- Losing interest in once-loved activities
- Isolating oneself from family and friends, not seeming to want to go out
- Drastically changing sleeping or eating patterns
- Acting in reckless or otherwise self-destructive ways (this can range from driving erratically to taking drugs or drinking too much)

Sometimes close friends can spot additional, subtler signs that something is wrong. If this is the case for you, I urge you to talk to your friend to earnestly try to find out how they're doing. And if a friend is discussing suicide—and certainly if they are at the point of mentioning specific plans—it is time to talk to a trusted adult. "Fixing" a suicidal individual's problems is far too much for a young person to bear; for this reason, it is best to share with a parent—your own or your friend's—or a teacher or counselor at school.

In some cases a friend who is confiding suicidal thoughts may swear you to secrecy. I understand that this creates a very difficult situation, as you do not want to feel you've betrayed your friend and violated their trust in you. You also don't want your friend to become angry with you.

If you ever face this situation, please keep in mind what you must weigh these potential consequences—temporary loss of trust—against losing your friend altogether. While it is true that your friend who is struggling may be upset with you for a period of time, that will pass; eventually, they will come to a healthy and stable enough place to see that you acted out of love and concern for them, and fences will be mended.

In the long run, you will never regret taking steps to ensure a friend's safety; it is all too easy to become plagued with regret and guilt if you hold your tongue and end up losing that friend.

* * *

I would now like to focus on what I consider some of the largest contributors to teenage depression, isolation, and suicide risk: bullying.

One day during the fourth grade, David confided in me that he was being bullied by a boy in his class. The boy would put an arm lock on David's neck during canteen breaks. David was raised not to resort to violence under any circumstances. As such, he did not retaliate, although he did attempt to push the boy away.

This had gone on for a while before he told me about it, although he said he had notified his teacher on a few occasions. Feeling troubled, I immediately made an appointment to see his teacher, a pleasant Jesuit brother I had met during the annual parent-teacher dialogue.

During my meeting with the teacher, I explained the problem. The teacher then said something that caused me further alarm. He said the bully was incorrigible and had been counseled and punished on several occasions because he had also violently abused others in the class. The parents of the victims had complained to the school. I asked why the boy had not been removed from the class. Obviously, I thought, they should ensure a safe environment.

The reply I got was even more shocking: "Please forgive him. We must be compassionate. We shall monitor his actions in the future."

This was especially distressing to hear coming from a guardian of the faith to which David, Sara, and I belonged. I could not understand how the issue was about forgiveness; I thought it was about a safe environment for the children. How is it that it's not a serious thing when children are violently abused in school, but if a man divorces his spouse, it's a very serious matter and he gets tagged on his baptism certificate as Divorced? The real issue was being ignored. The priorities shown here would later cause me to rethink some of my assumptions about church authority.

However, these strange and potentially harmful priorities do not occur only in religious schools—many young people have found the institutions in which they spend the better part of their lives unable—or unwilling—to protect them from bullies.

On the assurance of the good teacher that the matter was under control, I left the school and went home to brief David. He was understandably not relieved. A few days later, David informed me the bully had struck again. I telephoned the school and informed the teacher I was on my way to see him.

I guess the teacher's calm detachment in this matter finally got to me. Admittedly, I was an angry parent. No, that's not quite true; I was really *pissed off*. I said to him that if this abusive behavior was not dealt with appropriately right away, then I might have to take things into my hands and confront the bully myself. That got the teacher's attention. He could see I was absolutely serious. The school finally acted, and the bully never bothered David again. I never knew what the school did to cause him to stop, and I didn't want to know—but stop he did.

David did the right thing—he reported the abuse. We, his father and his school, failed to act urgently because we felt schoolyard bullying was normal. *It's just kids having a go at each other*, we thought. Nothing serious.

Please get out of this mindset. Schoolyard bullying is one of the most serious acts of abuse. Children are vulnerable and sensitive. They have dreams. A bully will cause the destruction of those dreams and possibly ruin the child's happiness *forever*.

David went through a traumatic period as a consequence of the bullying. No child should have to go through this. He suffered in silence. This is *not* a baptism by fire, as some idiots try to convince us. Do not accept bullying, under any circumstances. Report it to a parent, teacher, or a responsible adult. Do not live in fear. You have us behind you on this—the millions of people in this world who know what it is like to be bullied!

> *Do not accept bullying, under any circumstances. Report it to a parent, teacher, or a responsible adult. Do not live in fear. You have us behind you on this—the millions of people in this world who know what it is like to be bullied!*

* * *

In addition to the same types of turmoil teens have been dealing with for years, today's young people face new challenges—challenges that sometimes their parents, older siblings, and adult acquaintances are not well equipped to help them make it through.

As the world has evolved over the last thirty years toward a technological village, new forms of expression have been created. These have facilitated global and economic growth, learning, communications, and the general advancement of the human condition. The positive aspects of technology far outweigh its downside.

But I want to touch on how the individual, particularly the young individual, is to embrace new technologies in a way that empowers them and fulfills a need or desire for expression as a person. Everybody wants to be heard. Social media offers us that opportunity. Social media shows above all that we are individuals and are different from one another. Social media—that is, the global village—recognizes and respects this.

However, because we are individuals with zillions of personality traits, it may at times be challenging to accommodate those who feel a desire to express destructive feelings about others on social media. The one who expresses this is perhaps emotionally troubled, and the one who is targeted then becomes the victim of this unbalanced emotional state. In basic terms, the abuser is dragging the victim to her level of emotional distress—and worse. The consequences of this act cannot be overstated by any measure, since what had in the past taken place in the schoolyard is now transferred to an online environment. This move from physical to emotional or psychological abuse is attractive to the bully for three reasons:

1. It can be anonymous.

2. It is perceived as less injurious.

3. The pen is mightier than the sword.

Remember, every bully is a coward. They are driven by fear and envy. They are, in some ways, almost as much a victim of circumstances as the person they abuse. Social media, however, is generally unregulated. This is not a bad thing, since the alternative is Big Brother and then even *Bigger* Brother.

The cyberbully is a creature of insecurity. They try to be anonymous, and if that is not necessary, they overtly use their "pen" to destroy those whom they feel threaten their ego or self-image.

They think this is all right, as the abuse is nonphysical. This, as we know, can lead to tragic consequences, judging from the countless suicides of victims of cyberbullying.

Recognizing that schoolyard bullying has graduated to the cyber domain, what can be done to prevent this? There is no simple answer. The traditional solutions—parental and school supervision, disciplinary action, and so forth—have been used against schoolyard bullies since time immemorial, to no avail. David himself suffered on several occasions from schoolyard bullying, and the school did not take action until I left them with little choice. There are institutional weaknesses.

Until there is a clearer solution, I believe we must focus on open and honest communication. It is often up to families to establish an environment in which young people know they are free to confide in their parents about any difficulties they are experiencing.

It is up to us, as well—in regard to cyberbullying, schoolyard bullying, and simply how we relate to one another—to emphasize empathy. No matter how hard we try, we will never understand precisely what it's like to walk that proverbial mile in another's shoes—and this is all the more reason to constantly act with understanding and benignity.

A final letter from David's dear friend Liz:

14/1/2018

Dear David,

Typing up these letters have taught me a few things.

One is that I'll never, ever be able to understand why you left. And that I'll never stop feeling like I could have done something more.

Second, I feel like these letters are all about my feelings, and not about you at all. And that shouldn't be the case. This book is meant to be about you. It is for you. That's why I'm hesitant about sending these letters, because I don't want it to be about me.

I've decided to send these letters to your dad because he'll put you first, over anything. He'll do anything for you, as long as it's in your best interests. So I'll let him decide.

Finally, if there's something I've learnt, it's this. Thanks for teaching me the greatest life lesson of all—that I should never belittle someone's feelings and chose to say or do nothing. That I shouldn't rely on other people (and adults) to help you, when I could have done so much more. I'm your best friend. And I was crap at it.

It sucks that you're not here anymore. It really sucks. You're not here to experience all these new journeys that I've been going through and I feel so alone.

At the very least, I'm comforted by the fact that when I do die, at least there's someone on the other side, hopefully waiting for me. Maybe that's a really selfish thought, but I don't want to think that the 13th Feb 2016 would the last time I ever see you.

CONCLUSION

The Great Dictator, a 1940 film that Charlie Chaplin wrote, directed, produced, scored, and starred in, is a powerful denouncement of Hitler, the Nazis, and fascism. So much of Chaplin's final speech in the film is true about Singapore today. It is one of the final items I want to leave you with: a message that contains much of the same weight that it did almost eight decades ago, one that represents what David attempted to convey to the military representatives who refused to listen.

> To those who can hear me, I say: do not despair. The misery that is now upon us is but the passing of greed—the bitterness of men who fear the way of human progress. The hate of men will pass, and dictators die, and the power they took from the people will return to the people. And so long as men die, liberty will never perish ...
>
> Soldiers! don't give yourselves to brutes—men who despise you, enslave you, who regiment your lives, tell you what to do—what to think and what to feel! Who drill you, diet you, treat you like cattle, use you as cannon fodder. Don't give yourselves to these unnatural men—machine men with machine minds and machine hearts! You are not machines! You are not cattle! You are men! You have the love of humanity in your hearts! You don't hate!

Only the unloved hate—the unloved and the unnatural! Soldiers! Don't fight for slavery! Fight for liberty!

In the 17th Chapter of St Luke it is written: "the Kingdom of God is within man"—not one man nor a group of men, but in all men! In you! You, the people have the power—the power to create machines. The power to create happiness! You, the people, have the power to make this life free and beautiful, to make this life a wonderful adventure.

Then—in the name of democracy—let us use that power, let us all unite. Let us fight for a new world, a decent world that will give men a chance to work, that will give youth a future and in old age a security. By the promise of these things, brutes have risen to power. But they lie! They do not fulfill that promise. They never will!

Dictators free themselves but they enslave the people! Now let us fight to fulfill that promise! Let us fight to free the world, to do away with national barriers, to do away with greed, with hate and intolerance. Let us fight for a world of reason, a world where science and progress will lead to all men's happiness. Soldiers! In the name of democracy, let us all unite!

In David's absence, I must carry on this message. I will not fail him again.

* * *

As David's father, I have set out to create this book as a tribute to my son's legacy, as I will seek to fulfill any and all wishes he has conveyed to me. All the material I include here—all my own words about him—will never begin to describe the void in my life resulting from David's death. I have lost my beloved son and best friend, who constantly mentored me in the things that truly mattered. I walk in his footsteps.

In closing, I would like to share a poem I have written in honor of him. It is titled "A Daze I Go on my Journey." It was read at David's memorial service.

A DAZE I GO ON MY JOURNEY

A Daze I go on my journey
Wandering, and not knowing
If it's dark or sunny,

The contours ahead are a blur,
But the honeyed air is unmistakably Him.
The Pain is momentarily forgotten

For what the Eyes cannot see,
The Senses have gotten.

A daze I go on my journey.

In the Spirit of David Cornelius Singh

POSTSCRIPT

In June/July 2019, I visited New York City once again in remembrance of David and to attend the LGBTQI+ Pride celebrations, marking the fiftieth anniversary of the Stonewall uprising. This was my third annual visit since David's passing. Once again, I walked to Central Park to ride on the carousel, as David and his friend Kimi did in July of 2014.

David in July 2014 at the carousel in Central Park, New York City

David's father in May 2017 at the carousel in Central Park, New York City

Always in remembrance of David.

As the Diaspora Jews over the centuries prayed, "Next year, in Jerusalem," so it is for me:

"Next year, in New York."

---

www.ingramcontent.com/pod-product-compliance
Lightning Source LLC
Chambersburg PA
CBHW041126110526
44592CB00020B/2704